COUPONING

QuickStart Guide

SECOND EDITION

The Simplified Beginner's Guide to Couponing

ClydeBank FINANCE

Edition # 2 – Updated: August 22, 2016

Editor: Marilyn Burkley

Cover Illustration and Design: Katie Poorman, Copyright © 2016 by ClydeBank Media LLC
Interior Design: Katie Poorman, Copyright © 2016 by ClydeBank Media LLC

For information about bulk purchase discounts, please contact sales@clydebankmedia.com.

ClydeBank Media LLC
P.O Box 6561
Albany, NY 12206

Printed in the United States of America

Copyright © 2016
www.clydebankmedia.com
All Rights Reserved

ISBN-13 : 978-1-945051-44-9

contents

Terms displayed in **bold italic** can be found
defined in the glossary, starting on page 111.
&
Feel free to take notes beginning on page 114.

introduction

I first became intrigued by couponing in 2005. I'd recently graduated from college and was living in Columbia, Missouri. I was working two part-time jobs, one as a clerk at Barnes & Noble and another selling cell phones out of a kiosk at the mall. Though still unsure of my professional path, I had no shortage of energy and was attracted to entrepreneurism. In 2005 alone I'd conducted serious research into starting (or purchasing) a retail gelato business, a Segway touring business, and an online couponing business. As fate would have it, it was the lattermost endeavor, the couponing business, that attracted the most attention from my family, friends, and would-be partners. It wasn't that my other ideas (gelato and Segway tours) were bad. It was just that the couponing project—"Columbia Smart Shopper" as I'd initially named it—possessed an undeniable, slam-dunk value proposition.

The idea was to set up a website for grocery shoppers that allowed them to quickly identify local grocers offering great prices on sought-after items. Customers would build their grocery lists on the site and would immediately be told where to go to find the best deals in town.

What made the concept truly great, however, was the introduction of coupons. A friend and mentor of mine began looking into the emerging phenomenon of *IP (Internet printable)* coupons and concluded that if I could find an efficient way to match low regional sale prices with powerful coupon-based savings, the result would be a truly revolutionary, money-saving product for my customers.

I began building trial databases using the sales data from general grocery sale circulars that came in the mail. I contacted management-

and corporate-level staff at various grocery chains and tried to convince them it was in their interest to disclose their sales prices to me forty-eight hours before they were released to the public. I hired a bright web developer, and soon we had a beta version of the website up and running.

The beta site was, well, not great. My web developer was exceptionally bright but fresh out of school, like me, and inexperienced (also like me). And the concept, as I envisioned it, required a website with multiple levels of functionality, from ecommerce to automated database management. I didn't have the nerve or the know-how to scale the business appropriately, and I'd already spent a substantial amount of my own money on it.

A couple of weeks after launching the beta site, one of my part-time employers offered me a full-time salaried management position if I would agree to relocate to the St. Louis area. I took the job and bade farewell to Columbia Smart Shopper.

It was at some point between 2008 and 2009, shortly after the release of the iPhone 3G, when I discovered a website and a corresponding app called "The Grocery Game." Lo and behold, a California entrepreneur named Teri Gault had taken the same idea (my idea) and run with it.

Note : The Grocery Game closed its virtual doors in early 2016, but other similar "coupon-to-sale matching services," such as www.grocerycouponnetwork.com, have taken the same concept and carried it forward.

As the smartphone era took hold, a slew of other online/mobile couponing services were established; many of them found success. In 2013, online couponing company RetailMeNot went public, raising

---

[1] Lee Spears and Chelsey Dulaney, "RetailMeNot Surges in Initial Trading after $191 Million IPO," *Bloomberg* (July 2013): http://www.bloomberg.com/news/articles/2013-07-19/retailmenot-surges-after-pricing-191-million-ipo-at-mid-range

[2] "Mobile Couponing Statistics Demonstrate Virality," *TrueShip.* (July 2015): Accessed May 26, 2016, http://www.trueship.com/blog/2015/07/16/mobile-couponing-statistics-demonstrate-virality/#.V0eMxZErKM9

$191 million in capital through its initial public offering.[1] By 2014, about five hundred million people worldwide were using mobile coupons. That number is expected to surpass one billion by the year 2019.[2]

Who's to say where I'd be now had I spent the last ten years in the coupon industry? Perhaps we'd have merged with The Grocery Game or made deals with product manufacturers allowing us to issue our own coupons to customers. I wonder how much we might have raised during our own initial public offering.

Oh well, no regrets. Hindsight's always 20/20, but the fact remains, money-saving opportunities through coupons are more widespread and abundant than ever before, from your newspaper to your phone and everywhere in between. If you know where to look, how to organize, and how to think about couponing, then you're bound to find success.

Now, we've scanned high and low, far and wide, from hell to breakfast, and six ways from the Sunday funnies to track down the best coupons. We've also sought out and evaluated a multitude of time-saving coupon organizational systems that will ensure you get the maximum amount of money-saving coupon mileage with the least amount of time investment. And that last bit is important too: *how to think* about couponing. Remember, *coupons are marketing tools.* Coupons are not random acts of corporate kindness. A wise man once said, "Couponing is like sailing and coupons are like the wind. A good sailor is not blown about by the wind but harnesses its power, shaping it to his own chosen velocity."

Okay, full disclosure, the metaphor's my own creation. But still, the concept holds true, does it not? Coupons should complement your shopping habits and save you money. They should not radically alter your routine. This book will teach you how to save money by setting your own course with couponing. If you're looking to become an "Extreme Couponer," great; we'll introduce you to the simple and essential strategy that Extreme Couponers use to save several thousand dollars a year in groceries and consumer goods. If you'd prefer a more casual approach, then we'll show you everything you need to know and then some. If you're keen on a good deal, but don't want to spend exorbitant amounts of time cutting or printing coupons, again, we've got you covered. If you're interested in what the online universe has to offer when it comes to coupons and deals, and would prefer to minimize your clipping in favor of a few solid apps, again, this QuickStart Guide will be your essential couponing companion.

In the first chapter we're going to introduce you to **the four kinds of couponers**. They come from different types of households and have different goals when it comes to couponing. See if you can find yourself!

| 1 |

Goal Setting & Soul Searching

In This Chapter

- Understanding why goal setting is ESSENTIAL to good couponing
- Why you should first understand couponing as an art before trying to make it into a science
- Defining the four different types of couponers
- Why couponing is not a remedy for extreme poverty and why you should avoid couponing out of desperation
- What is meant by "Extreme Couponing"
- Couponing while receiving social/government assistance

Even though this chapter is labeled Chapter 1, we actually created it last. Following our thorough research into the subject of couponing, after sharing our own experiences and those of others, after discovering all of the unique couponing tools, services, and publications, and after listening to the advice of the "couponing gurus," one thing became abundantly clear: couponing is not a one-size-fits-all activity. In order for you to achieve the ongoing, money-saving, budget-lengthening success with couponing that you desire, you must first define your goals and, to some extent, search your soul.

DO NOT SKIP THIS CHAPTER. Though you may be tempted many times in this chapter to rush ahead to the "how" of couponing, it is imperative that you first understand your own personal motivation and commitment level; the "why" of couponing. I've got news for you: it's a lot more complicated than "I want to save money."

Couponing Is First & Foremost an Art, Not a Science

Don't underestimate the complexity of couponing. It can be at once rewarding, frustrating, time-consuming, socially awkward, complicated, challenging, easy, difficult, fun, and futile. You're not going to be in the right place at the right time to capitalize on every great deal. You're not always going to make it to the store before the expiration date. There will be times when you go out of your way to chase down a deal only to find that the shelf has been stripped bare by other shoppers. When you show up at the checkout line with a fistful of coupons, cashiers and the customers queued up behind you may give you stink eye as you save hundreds of dollars at checkout. The joke's on them, right? Sure, but it's still awkward. You're going to have to wade through a multitude of coupon offers that are not worth the paper they're printed on even though they look appealing. You're going to have to organize, strategize, plot, plan, and execute. You will need to be flexible, agile, smart, determined, and patient. And, most fundamentally, you must have a clear idea of what you want to gain from your efforts. Good couponing practices are heavily dependent on establishing a sound goal-oriented strategy up front. Failing to take the time to establish such a strategy can lead to confusion, indecision, over-analysis, frustration, and can ultimately drive would-be couponers to despair and quit.

In this chapter, we're going to walk you through an introspective process for establishing objectives that will culminate in a sound personalized strategy. Let's begin by introducing you to the four types of couponers.

The graphic (Figure 1) illustrates four principal couponing types based on a combination of factors. The first defining factor is the couponer's principal motivation. It's safe to say that if you're reading this book, then you're interested in saving money. However, it's important to acknowledge that "saving money" can mean a lot of different things to different households. Defining your "type" allows you to employ

fig. 1

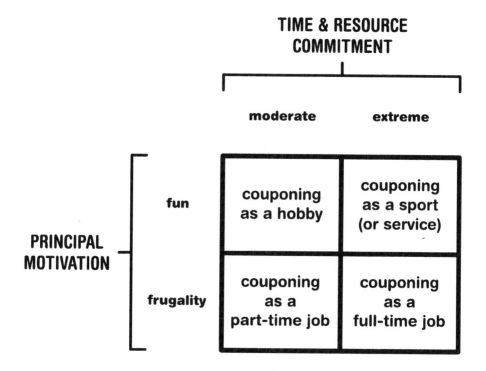

situation-specific guiding principles when making decisions. For example, some couponers may wish to purchase multiple subscriptions of the Sunday newspaper in order to have multiple copies of coupons on hand. Other couponers would rather not spread their grocery shopping out beyond one or two favorite stores.

Many couponers, when assessing their level of flexibility, their principal focus, and so forth, are quick to assert that "It all depends on what deals are available." For example, if you're aware of an amazing deal at a grocery store that you're otherwise not so fond of, then sure, you'd be willing to make a one-time visit. My response to this is yes, of course you're going to factor in the quality of the offers that are available to you at any given time, but for the moment you don't know what offers are coming down the pipe, all you know about is your current situation. And I'm here to tell you that carefully taking stock of your current situation is critical if you want to make real progress as a couponer.

Frugal/Extreme Couponer: "Money Saver on a Mission"

Let's pay a visit to the household of Jeannie Weisman. Jeannie is a stay-at-home mom with two beautiful children, aged four and seven. Her husband Frank is a middle school math and science teacher and brings home a modest income. Recently Jeannie has been becoming more and more worried about financial matters. Though Frank's income is sufficient to make ends meet, no money is being put aside for college expenses, and retirement contributions are minimal. Jeannie doesn't want to send her four-year-old to daycare but would gladly do anything in her power to provide a substantial boost to family finances. She is prepared to make a serious commitment to frugality when it comes to shopping and finding the best deals. She's prepared to be incredibly flexible and to spend significant amounts of time, and she's dead set on procuring savings for her family on a scale that can change their lives. Though no one says Jeannie can't have fun with her new "job" as a couponer, her principal motivation is frugality. And her commitment level is high, or, as they say in couponing circles, she is ready to become an "extreme couponer." In Figure 1, Jeannie falls into the bottom right-hand section of the quadrant, a frugal/extreme couponer.

The frugal extreme (FrE) couponer's guiding principles are something akin to the following:

- FrEs create and maintain a complex and thorough coupon organizing system (Chapter 4).

- FrEs may be willing to devote significant amounts of storage space to stockpiling nonperishable food or goods that can be obtained at high quantities for low prices.

- FrEs will seek out the best possible sources for coupons (so as to best fit their shopping needs) regardless of whether these sources are print-based, mobile/Internet, rewards-based, etc. (Chapter 2).

- FrEs will adjust their shopping schedules in order to capitalize on sale dates and "double-coupon days." When possible they will shop during the early hours on weekdays, when stores are the least busy. Otherwise they may have to endure the disapproving looks of annoyed cashiers or other shoppers at checkout.

- FrEs will make strategic investments in various types of collateral if they believe it enhances their ability to maximize coupon savings. They may purchase multiple subscriptions to the newspaper, or they may ask friends and family members to "donate" coupons received by mail, through subscription services, or through rewards-based purchases.

- FrEs are the savviest of all couponers when it comes to identifying "bad" coupons. In most cases, they will gladly purchase a house brand or generic if it is less expensive than a name brand that has been marginally discounted via a "bad coupon" (Chapter 5).

- FrEs are the most highly disciplined of all couponers. They will not under any circumstances allow a low price (provided by a sale or a coupon) to goad them into making an unnecessary purchase. FrEs are cautious and skeptical and have no illusions about the reality of couponing: that a coupon's raison d'etre is not to save consumers money but to market products. FrEs beat the marketers at their own game.

- FrEs use traditional channels as well as social media (Chapter 7) to build powerful networks with other couponers. They share tips and news alerts about various offers.

- FrEs, to the best of their ability, employ more sophisticated methods and invest in services (such as coupon-to-sale matching services, Chapter 5) that will help them zero in on the most promising money-saving opportunities.

- If FrEs approach crowd-sourced couponing opportunities (Chapter 2), it is with a full awareness that the majority of the offers are for nonessential items and services. FrEs who choose to use crowd-sourced couponing will set up product-specific alerts and filters so that they're only notified when essential items are featured.

Fun/Extreme Couponer: "Master of the Couponing Universe"

The fun/extreme couponer (FuE) has a lot in common with the frugal/extreme couponer, but not everything. A good example of a fun/extreme couponer is a person who is happy devoting a significant amount of time and technique to couponing, but who is ultimately not depending on coupon-based savings for the procurement of essential financial goals. The FuE couponer doesn't need to be as vigilant against bad coupons. He may be giving away huge swaths of his take to charities in need of canned foods, or food banks that store and give away perishable food items to the poor in the community. Perhaps he's interested in authoring a blog on couponing so he can share his techniques with others. Whatever the case may be, the FuE couponer is incredibly savvy with couponing (like the FrE), but views it more like a sport or a vehicle by which he can provide a service to others.

The FuE's guiding principles are essentially the same as the FrE's, with the following amendments:

- The FuE may take a much more thorough interest in crowd-sourced coupons and other unconventional couponing techniques (Chapter 8). He sees these methods as the cutting edge of couponing and wants to make sure that he maintains his expertise.

- The FuE, though aware of the marketing undercurrents that belie the apparent money-saving promises of couponing, may be perfectly happy to purchase a product he'd not normally buy or try a higher-end brand even if its post-coupon expense is greater than the generic equivalent.

- Networking is a must-do for the FuE couponer, and it's not just about getting info on deals. It's through their networks that FuE couponers gage their standings and achievements within the world of couponing. FuEs use their networks to promote their blogs, Twitter accounts, and other assets that help enshrine their mastery of the couponing craft.

Fun/Moderate Couponer: "Just Looking for a Good Time"

The fun/moderate (FuM) couponer views couponing as simply a hobby. He's not going to stress himself out to ensure that his couponing efforts are efficient to the utmost. He's not going to devote a specific closet in his house to stockpiling macaroni and cheese boxes. Neither is he likely to adopt a tedious and complex organizational structure to track his couponing pursuits. The fun/moderate couponer is a person who loves to shop and also loves getting great deals.

The FuM's guiding principles are a lot less rigid than those of any other couponer.

- The FuM sources coupons through media that he enjoys consuming. If he doesn't enjoy reading the Sunday paper, then you probably won't find him wielding coupons found in the Sunday paper.

- Like the FuE couponer, the FuM is more inclined to use crowd-sourced coupons and other unconventional couponing methods to the extent that they suit his innate interest.

- Unlike the FuE, the FuM doesn't feel as if he needs to be on the cutting edge of couponing. His main motivation for reading a book like this one is to gather a few extra tips, tricks, and insights into the world of couponing.

- If the FuM is a social person, then he'll pursue networking opportunities with other couponers. Otherwise, he's more or less content to pursue his hobby quietly.

Frugal/Moderate Couponer: "It's All About Efficiency"

This is the category most likely to encompass the majority of readers of this book. In many ways the frugal/moderate (FrM) couponer's principles are scaled down versions of those listed under frugal/extreme. FrM couponers, like FrEs, are more money-savers than shoppers. They value efficiency in couponing because they don't have all day to spend on it. They are most likely reading this book with the objective of getting more mileage out of their couponing efforts.

Many FrMs believe that the more they diversify and complicate their approach to couponing, the more time and energy they'll end up losing. They're not big on chasing sales or stocking their homes to the brim with goods for which they have no regular need.

FrMs aren't so rigid about their couponing that they refuse to visit new grocery stores or militantly stick to their preferred brands. They proceed always with practicality in mind, looking for simple actions they can take to save money without turning couponing into their new full-time job.

The guiding principles of the FrM couponer are as follows:

- FrM couponers want to save money through couponing but want the money saved to be worth the expense in time and effort. They don't want to spend countless hours organizing or learning new technologies or systems for very little payoff.

- The FrM is interested in organizational systems that will boost his couponing efficiency (Chapter 4).

- FrMs will consider using FrE tactics, such as maintaining multiple newspaper subscriptions, only if they see a clear and regular return on their investment.

- An FrM will purchase in bulk when a good opportunity presents itself and will, to a reasonable extent, store nonperishables at home so long as they are frequently used items.

- The FrM couponer carefully selects networking opportunities on the basis of their ability to provide efficient value.

Couponers Come in Many Colors

You, of course, have your own unique circumstances and may not fit in perfectly with any of the couponing archetypes described in this chapter. As an exercise, try to answer the following questions about your goals for couponing, and then plot your position on the chart that follows:

1. Ideally, how many hours a week would I like to spend couponing (estimate)?

2. Am I willing to shop at stores at which I'd not normally shop? To what extent? Are there any stores that I absolutely will not shop in?

3. To what extent am I willing to investigate and try out new couponing services, mobile apps, and websites?

4. To what extent am I willing to use space in my home for storage of nonperishable goods purchased at a deep discount? Would the promise of saving substantial amounts of money be my primary motivation for stockpiling, or am I motivated by other reasons, such as charity, competition, or to establish a high-level expertise?

5. Am I interested in sharing ideas and news about couponing with other couponers? Am I more inclined to pursue networking opportunities through traditional means? Social media? Or am I simply focused on networking wherever there's the most value to be had?

fig. 2

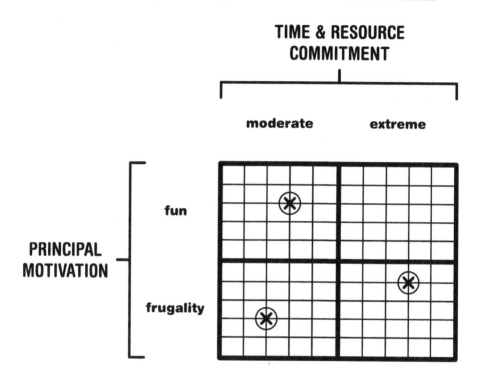

Which Type of Couponer Are You?

TIME & RESOURCE COMMITMENT

moderate   extreme

PRINCIPAL MOTIVATION

fun

frugality

Now that you've asked yourself some important questions about what you expect to achieve and what you're willing (and not willing) to do with regard to your pursuit of couponing, take a moment to mark your place on the grid displayed in Figure 2. We've added three sample positions to illustrate the idea.

Once you've identified where you fit within the spectrum of couponers, it will be easier for you to make quick decisions that will support your overall couponing strategy. For example, let's say you come across a coupon for twenty cents off a sixteen-ounce container of Febreze® fabric spray. You use Febreze® regularly, but you routinely purchase the thirty-ounce rather than the sixteen-ounce quantity. At a glance you're not sure if using the twenty cents off coupon will offset the slightly higher base price you'd pay for purchasing the smaller per-ounce quantity.

The couponer with more moderate tendencies (FuM or FrM), will probably disregard the coupon altogether or will print or cut it out and file it into his basic couponing system (Chapter 4) if it has at least 30 days before expiration.

The couponer who identifies more as an extreme type (FuE or FrE) will first retrieve his carefully organized stockpile of grocery store receipts, verify the average per-ounce purchase price of the thirty-ounce Febreze® product (the one he routinely purchases), and will then write down (on the coupon) the highest allowable price that the sixteen-ounce Febreze® can be in order for the coupon to be valuable (the per-ounce price of the sixteen-ounce product with coupon must be lower than the standard per-ounce price of the thirty-ounce product. On the extreme couponer's next trip to the store—preferably one that has an advertised weekly sale price on sixteen-ounce Febreze®, and one that eminently meets the value threshold for the coupon—he'll use as many copies of the coupon as he can to capitalize on the uniquely low per-ounce price of the product. Afterward he'll return home and pad his likely already surging stockpile of deeply discounted Febreze®.

You can find success in couponing regardless of how extreme or moderate you intend to be. What's important is that you set an intention that's appropriate for your financial objectives and the amount of time and energy you're comfortable committing. Identifying your type and setting your intention and your limits will help you advance with steadiness toward your goals.

Avoid Couponing out of Desperation

As a final note on this chapter, before we move into the more technical, how-to dimensions of this text, it's important to understand the limits of couponing. Couponing can be a powerful form of financial *supplement*, but should not be looked at as a form of financial *sustenance*.

Consider the true story of Joni Meyer-Crothers, a single mother who found herself divorced with three young children to take care of. During her time of struggle, she was confronted with choices at the grocery store that no one should be forced to make, such as whether to purchase toothpaste for her children or feminine hygiene products. In her own account of this difficult time she writes, "We couldn't afford to purchase both. I put tissue in my pants when I was on my monthly cycle so my kids could brush their teeth."[3]

Joni's situation was clearly one of extreme need, and it's worth nothing that she did not attempt to resolve her situation by couponing but by first finding a way to bring more income into her household. It wasn't until later on in her life, after things had stabilized significantly, that Joni began developing her skills as a master couponer.

Joni's case illustrates an important point. While couponing can be a powerful asset for frugal-minded people, it's not a direct remedy for poverty. Saving significant sums of money with couponing involves subjecting oneself to the whims of marketers and beating them at their own games. It means occasionally buying more of a product than you need and storing it away for future use. It means waiting for the right day to buy certain products so that you can capitalize on the best possible prices. In many respects, the successful couponer sacrifices flexibility in order to save money in the long run. It is a dynamic that's wholly incompatible with the day-by-day struggles of poverty, where one's ability to be as flexible as possible and to meet pressing needs quickly is paramount. The single parent with hungry children isn't interested

---

[3] Joni Meyer-Crothers, *Extreme Couponing* (New York: Penguin 2013), 4.

in buying multiple twelve-packs of paper towels (even at an amazing price) when there's no food in the house. This person's efforts are much better spent finding ways to generate more income.

Even our more frugal-minded couponers must operate out of a flexible base of operations in order to find meaningful success.

Silencing the Coupon Siren Song

One of the reasons couponing is not a viable remedy for poverty is the undeniable ability of certain coupons to induce many shoppers to actually spend more than they would have spent without any coupons at all. As an example, some stores, such as Bed, Bath & Beyond and Michael's, regularly issue coupons for 15 or 20 percent off that can be applied not just to one item but to entire purchases. I discovered this phenomenon through the shopping app, RetailMeNot, during a trip to Michael's to pick up some crafting supplies. The cashier was happy to scan the coupon right off my phone for a quick 20 percent discount. For me, a person who doesn't regularly shop at Michael's, this coupon did little more than put some extra money in my pocket. But for others, such as my fiancée, who can lose entire days (it seems) wandering the aisles of a Michael's or a Bed, Bath & Beyond, these across-the-board coupons can be, well, dangerous.

I call it the coupon siren song, an enchanted and financially disastrous melody that lures shoppers into feeling as if they should purchase more than what they actually need, because they're "getting a great deal!"

Other coupons accomplish similar ends by getting consumers to try something new, expensive, and potentially unneeded. The pet food company Purina did this recently with a new line of organic cat food that, though much more costly than standard cat food, was made to look like "a great deal!" thanks to the siren song of the many coupons used to promote the new brand during its launch. In the words of the authors of a 2013 New York University study on coupon users, "A coupon decreases the unattractiveness of high price by framing the price as a mixed gain rather than as a net loss."[4] And I have to admit, I fell hook, line, and sinker for Purina's ploy; now my cat eats like a king.

Silencing the coupon siren song is not easy. If you want to succeed you have to keep your head on your shoulders and always remember your original intent and goals as a couponer. Later on in this book (Chapter 4) we will go into depth on the practice of buffering yourself against unneeded purchases by promptly throwing away coupons for products that you don't need or don't want to purchase.

What is Meant by "Extreme Couponing"

We use the term "extreme" to define two of the main couponing types featured in this chapter. The notion of "extreme couponing" may sound familiar to you. The main claim to fame of "Extreme Couponing" is that it is the title of a TLC television show that first aired in 2009.[5] Given that more eccentricity leads to better ratings, the tactics depicted on the "Extreme Couponing" television show go above and beyond what most normal people would consider adopting to further their couponing objectives. Perhaps more importantly, the show has come under criticism for offering an unrealistic depiction of the average store's level of receptivity toward couponers. Store owners have even gone on record confessing that their stores allowed certain instances of *double couponing* only while the show was being filmed.[6] A regular consumer armed with the same coupons would not be able to realize the same savings.

---

[4] Manoj Thomas, Kapil Bawa, and Geeta Menon, "Spending More to Save More: The Impact of Coupons on Premium Priced Products" (academic paper, NYU, 2003), 1, http://pages.stern.nyu.edu/~gmenon/Coupons.pdf

[5] "Extreme Couponing," *The Learning Channel* (December 2009): http://www.imdb.com/title/tt1836419/

[6] Jacqueline Curtis, "The Myths of TLC's 'Extreme Couponing' – How Couponing Really Works," *MoneyCrashers.com*: Accessed May 17, 2016.

Nevertheless, the show was at least partially based on reality, and for highly ambitious couponers the "extreme" method can be very effective.

Three of the hallmarks of extreme couponing are 1) a willingness to purchase an abnormally large stock of items when the price is right, 2) a willingness to regularly travel across multiple shopping venues in order to maximize savings on a broad array of products, and 3) a willingness to invest significant amounts of time into the acquisition, organization, and strategic use of coupons.

Extreme Couponing Hazards

TLC's depiction of extreme couponing features shoppers who, by collecting hundreds, if not thousands of coupons, are able to walk away from a grocery store with thousands of dollars of food and other items for free. While such a feat may still be possible—even in light of the special TV-only privileges enjoyed by the show's protagonists—this level of extreme couponing requires a time commitment virtually equal to a full-time job. On the bright side, if you've been seduced by "the extreme," then it won't be too difficult to find your couponing type. You're either a fun/extreme couponer or a frugal/extreme couponer, depending on your principal motivation (see Figure 1).

Extreme couponers with a tendency to hoard should be forewarned: A shopper that journeys too deep down the couponing rabbit hole may reemerge as a bona fide hoarder. Once you invest your energy in the cause of extreme coupon savings, you may find it difficult to pass up the opportunity to acquire ten-cent jars of Tabasco sauce by the pallet-full. As couponer and blogger Vera Sweeney puts it, "Are you willing to give up your entire basement for some BBQ sauce?"[7]

Such *extreme* forms of extreme couponing are simply not practical for the average consumer; not everyone has a few spare bedrooms

---

[7] http://www.ladyandtheblog.com/2011/01/05/what-is-extreme-couponing-how-can-i-get-started/

to devote to the storage of stocked goods or the time required to collect thousands of coupons, or any interest in maintaining (and paying for) five subscriptions to the same local newspaper all for the purpose of stockpiling coupons and the products they help procure. Another potential drawback to the extreme approach to couponing is the tendency of extreme couponers to purchase (or obtain for free or nearly free) large quantities of unhealthy products that they'd not otherwise purchase. Unfortunately, the best coupons aren't always for the healthiest of products, and if you're cultivating a process that's driven primarily by capitalizing on available deals, then you may find it's easy to let your health goals and good judgment slip to the back burner. For the more moderately-inclined couponers, though they may on occasion borrow from the tactical library of the extreme couponer, their main focus will be on the development of a pragmatic strategy that can be applied in a simple and timely manner. That said, even the moderate couponer might do well to study the extreme couponer's tools and methods. Later, when circumstances develop in which an "extreme" tactic can be exercised prudently, with minimal time commitment, then the moderate couponer will be ready to pounce.

Couponing on Social Assistance

Being on government funded social assistance does not prevent you from being a great couponer. People who are on fixed incomes often find themselves hard pressed to get as much mileage as they can get out of their spending allotments. Proficient couponing is one highly effective way to expand the purchasing capacity of individuals on fixed incomes. There are also specialized "welfare coupons" issued to persons in qualifying circumstances. One such welfare coupon issuing agency is WIC (Women, Infants, and Children), which provides grocery coupons for the purchase of staple food items such as bread, cheese, eggs, and milk.

To Recap

- The mechanics of couponing are highly personality-specific. It is much more of an art than a science.

- The key factors that determine your "type" as a couponer are the extent to which your efforts at couponing are designed to address serious financial challenges and the extent to which you're prepared to commit time and resources to your couponing efforts.

- There are four essential types of couponers: Frugal/Extreme, Fun/Extreme, Fun/Moderate, and Frugal/Moderate. Knowing where you fit within these essential types is critical to your ability to strategize, organize, and navigate your couponing pursuits.

- Though couponing tactics can save significant sums of money, the lack of predictability and flexibility inherent in couponing makes it unsuitable as a remedy for extreme poverty.

- Beware the couponing siren song. Many coupons, for a variety of reasons, can induce the consumer to actually spend more than they'd have spent had they not used any coupons at all.

- "Extreme Couponing" is an idea made famous by a television show on the TLC channel. The show has come under fire for its heavily hyped depiction of jaw-dropping coupon savings that, in reality, are not always accessible or practical for the everyday couponer.

- Individuals on social/government assistance are in no way prohibited from using coupons.

| 2 |

The Origin, Mechanics, & Varieties

In This Chapter

- The first recorded use of a coupon
- The different issuers and types of coupons
- The life cycle of a coupon
- How online and mobile coupons are changing the game
- The crowd-sourced coupon business model

Couponing is an excellent method of saving money on products that you use every day. With the cost of goods (most importantly, food) increasing significantly in recent years, couponing will enable you to provide for yourself and your family in difficult times without having to go without. Taking advantage of significant savings with coupons will require some work, but with new forms of coupons tied to new technologies like the Internet and mobile devices, some of the required work will be much easier. Besides saving money, coupons may also introduce you to products, services, and savings you may never have known about.

Brief History of Couponing

A coupon is defined as an "official document exchanged for financial discount or rebate when purchasing a product."

Coupons were first used by the Coca-Cola Company in 1888. Coca-Cola employees and sales representatives were given special paper vouchers for a single free Coke to give to family, friends, and acquaintances. As an ingenious advertising and marketing tool, the

Coke coupons were designed to introduce potential customers to Coca-Cola by offering them a chance to "try before they buy." As fate would have it, it was a remarkable success. Between 1894 and 1913, one in nine Americans received a free Coke, and the Coca-Cola Company was on its way to becoming the international success that it is today. Presently, approximately 2,800 consumer-packaged goods companies offer coupons for discounted products, providing US consumers with an estimated annual savings of $4.6 billion.

fig. 3

Figure 3 features the first recorded coupon ever used. It was issued in 1888 to promote the Coca-Cola soft drink. The Coca-Cola company provided free syrup to distributors as a part of their campaign, and soon the iconic soft drink was being served in every US state.[8]

Coupon Terminology & Basics

To product manufacturers and local stores, the coupon is a powerful marketing and advertising tool. To the consumer, coupons are a gateway to smarter shopping strategies and significant savings. Marketers as well are very interested in coupons, regularly employing them in market research. Evaluating a product for "price sensitivity" is one among many real-world marketing studies made possible by coupons. It involves

---

[8] The Coca-Cola Company, "The Chronicle of Coca-Cola: The Candler Era," *Coca-ColaCompany.com* (January 2012): http://www.coca-colacompany.com/stories/the-chronicle-of-coca-cola-the-candler-era

testing a product at various prices among different groups of buyers; different dollar amounts are assigned to different groups of "shopper profiles" in order to determine the most effective way to market and sell a new or existing product.

There are two major broad categories of coupons: ***store coupons***, which are honored by a particular retailer, like a grocery store, and ***manufacturer coupons***, which are offered by the company that produces the product. Manufacturer coupons are produced in partnership with a ***coupon clearinghouse***, a separate company that assists in the creation, collections, and reimbursements necessary to properly execute a coupon-based promotion. The two largest and most well-known coupon clearinghouses are Valassis and News America Marketing, both of which produce coupon *"**circulars**,"* newspaper inserts that feature coupons and other promotions for several retailers. Coupons are redeemable in most places where the featured product is sold. After the coupons are used at a store, they are returned to the clearinghouse. The clearinghouse reimburses the store, then prepares an invoice to send to the manufacturer, adding a small commission fee for each redeemed coupon.

fig. 4

The Life Cycle of a Manufacturer Coupon

reimbursement is requested

coupon is printed/posted/distributed

clearinghouse

manufacturer

SHOP

customers

coupon is redeemed

Manufacturer coupons are used more frequently than store-issued coupons for the purposes of marketing and advertising, providing the consumer with an incentive to buy (and try) a product (as was the case with Coca-Cola's original coupon).

The beauty of having coupons issued by the manufacturer is that many grocery stores don't care how many coupons you use, as long as they are legitimate coupons and not fraudulent (more on that in Chapter 5). For example, say I have twenty legitimate copies of a manufacturer coupon for three dollars off a twelve-pack of toilet paper that would normally sell for six dollars. As long as the store had adequate stock, I could buy twenty twelve-packs for three dollars each, saving a grand total of sixty dollars. Twenty coupons may sound like a lot, but in the more "extreme" circles of couponing, twenty coupons is child's play.

> *Note : In Chapter 5 we'll talk about preordering products at retailers to ensure that they have adequate quantity on hand for your purchase.*

Store coupons differ from manufacturer coupons in that stores publish coupons based on available inventory, sales cycles for perishable goods, or for a variety of other reasons. Some stores may even honor store coupons issued by their competitors.

> *Note : Individual store policies will affect your ability to leverage coupons of all types. Be aware of store-set limitations and opportunities, such as "**double-coupon day**" (see Chapter 5).*

Types of Coupons

Now that you understand the two broad categories of coupons, let's have a look at the four major types of coupons; these separate types refer to the method by which they're distributed: printed coupons, rewards-based coupons, online coupons, and mobile coupons.

Printed Coupons

Most people are already familiar with *printed coupons*, as these are coupons printed in traditional media like newspapers and magazines and sometimes distributed via mass mailings to homes within a certain geographical radius of a store. Generally speaking, printed coupons require more work to acquire and organize compared to digital coupons (online and mobile).

Online & Mobile Coupons

Online coupons are increasingly becoming the most convenient go-to source for couponing. Even if you've not yet used online coupons yourself, you've surely been standing in a checkout line somewhere and watched the cashier scan a barcode or QR code on another customer's phone. Online coupons may either be scanned directly off a mobile device or they may be printed out and presented at checkout. Online coupons may be emailed or sent to you via social media following your participation in a rewards-based program or a product subscription. It is safe to say that online and mobile coupons can be generated and used in all the same ways as regular and print coupons, but they offer an added level of usefulness in that they can be accessed and stored on a mobile device.

Note : It is not correct to say that online/mobile coupons are the only type of coupon that can be used for online shopping, because print coupons often provide checkout codes that can be entered electronically.

Online coupons are game-changers. There was a time when the *coupon circular* (the booklets that come by mail from companies like Valassis and RedPlum) would theoretically drive the decision of the consumer with regard to shopping venues. If your RedPlum circular contained coupons for Closet World, promising amazing prices on items you were interested in, then you'd certainly be inclined to visit

Closet World rather than a competing retailer. With the advent of mobile-based coupon services such as RetailMeNot (see Chapter 7), the coupon-savvy consumer is now inclined to choose their preferred venue and then scan their smartphone's coupon apps on-site for any available deals. Coupon issuing apps will most always be accessed using an Android or iOS (iPhone) smartphone or tablet device offering couponing applications. Some of these apps, like RetailMeNot, are third-party apps spanning a whole range of stores and products. Other coupon-issuing apps will be sponsored by individual retailers or manufacturers.

Rewards-Based Coupons

Have you ever had a cashier hand you a freshly printed coupon along with your receipt following a purchase? What you received is known as a rewards-based coupon. Rewards-based coupons are offered to individual customers as a result of their spending habits associated with a store loyalty ID card scanned in the checkout line. A reward coupon or a set of reward coupons may be issued after a certain quantity and/or a certain type of item is purchased. For example, if you purchase a bag of cat food, you may trigger a reward coupon for another cat-related product such as cat treats or more cat food. These types of reward coupons are designed to keep the shopper coming back to the store on a regular basis, while the main function of a reward card is to track purchases and provide valuable marketing data to the store (in addition to keeping the shopper engaged by the promise of deals and discounts made available by using the card).

Crowd-Sourced Couponing

It's been several years, but I remember the first time a friend posted a "Groupon" offer on my Facebook page. On the surface, the deal appeared nearly too good to be true, promising something like 50 percent off a meal at a local Japanese steakhouse. But once I did a little reading into the coupon-issuing agent, Groupon, I saw the logic. I even shared the coupon with several of my Facebook friends. I followed up personally with a few of them to get their reaction, and by and large, they thought the offer I sent them was some kind of spam, and they ignored it after subjecting it to their own personal "too good to be true" intellectual filter.

The funny thing about Groupon, and other companies that offer "crowd-sourced coupons," is that the offers made are, in many instances, genuinely awesome.

Note : The term "crowd-sourced coupons" was coined by ClydeBank Media in light of the fact that there doesn't appear to be any universally used name for this particular coupon type.

Here's how it works: Groupon makes a deal with a retailer whereby they (Groupon) commit to selling a certain number of coupons advertising a deep discount. For instance, in the case of the Japanese steakhouse, the coupon is sold for twenty-five dollars but is redeemable for fifty dollars at the restaurant. Hence, in theory, it operates like a 50 percent off coupon assuming a dinner expense of fifty dollars. Part of the deal between Groupon and the retailer (and the consumer) is that in order for the deal to "go active," it must be purchased by a particular quantity of consumers. If I sign up for the Japanese steakhouse deal—twenty-five dollars for the fifty-dollar coupon—and not enough other consumers sign up for the same deal, then the coupon isn't issued and I'm not charged. In most cases, however, the quota is met and the deal goes active. Groupon takes a commission for the sale value of all the coupons, the consumer gets a deeply discounted purchase, and the retailer gets a chance to show off their product and push for add-on and recurring business. As About.com writer Paul Gil puts it, "It's a very powerful win–win situation for all three parties."[9] Nevertheless, Groupon and its competitors have had to brave several pitfalls, often in the form of consumer frustrations, inherent in their business model. Moreover, especially for couponers who hold frugality as their most important guiding principle (Chapter 1), crowd-sourced couponing isn't always the best choice for reducing overall spending. We'll review some of these problem areas in more depth and will discuss best practices for crowd-sourced couponing in Chapter 6.

No doubt the advent of the mobile coupon and crowd-sourced couponing has had profound strategic implications for coupon-issuing manufacturers and retailers, as well as for marketing communications companies such as Valassis. The goal of this book, however, is not to advise businesses on how to best leverage coupons in the digital era, but to help you, the consumer. With the modern abundance of both print and electronic coupon-issuing agents, the savvy couponer is well poised to save tremendous amounts of money.

---

[9] Paul Gil, "Groupon: What Is 'Groupon'? How Does Groupon Work?" About.com (March 2016): http://netforbeginners.about.com/od/guidesfavorites/f/What-Is-Groupon-How-Does-Groupon-Work.htm

To Recap

- The first coupon was issued by the Coca-Cola Company in 1888.

- Coupons are issued by either manufacturers or retailers (stores).

- Coupons can be printed, rewards-based, online, or mobile. Print, online, and mobile coupons may also be rewards-based.

- Crowd-sourced coupons offer a powerful sales proposition, one that's mutually advantageous for both businesses and consumers. However, crowd sourcing doesn't always integrate well into a frugality-focused couponing strategy.

| 3 |

Coupons & Your Shopping Habits

In This Chapter
- Analyzing and tracking your shopping habits and budgets

There are different methods of acquiring and organizing coupons that will suit different budgeting and couponing approaches. Circular publications are found in newspapers and mailings, or sometimes even at retail stores, and are the most common sources of traditional printed coupons. Rewards-based coupons will be harder to obtain (and duplicate) since they require the purchase of other items, but they should also be considered a separate source of original coupons. Online and mobile coupons are often easier to find by simply using an online search engine or downloading a mobile application.

Equally important to collecting coupons is the organization method used to process your coupon collection and keep track of potential savings, including expiration dates. There are a variety of different organizational approaches to consider, but you shouldn't get bogged down in deliberation. You'll find more success and less frustration if you choose a system that reasonably accommodates your couponing "type" and stick with it for a while.

Before we get into the thick of where and how to acquire coupons, it's important that we first take some time to get a good handle on our shopping budget and the types of items we purchase most often. For those of you who just can't wait to learn all about where to find the best coupons, feel free to jump ahead to the "Finding Good Coupons" section, but be forewarned. You're about to enter the world of the marketers, and you'll be much better prepared if you first take the time to assess your budget and your current spending habits.

Existing & Projected Shopping Budgets

There are a few steps involved in designing a couponing system that will match your budget and shopping habits. We recommend beginning by doing a thorough assessment of your budget, followed by a defined tracking period, whereby you can get an idea of how much you're actually spending on a monthly basis for various items. Let's walk through some budget categories and results of tracking systems that are particularly relevant to couponing. Afterward, we'll take a look at a free online service that makes it easy to track your spending.

Groceries

Though effective couponing is by no means limited to the grocery store, there's no denying that the bulk of the coupons used by the average couponer are grocery-related.

Here's the good news: the average household's grocery budget generally tends to be stable. Unless there is a new member of your family or a dramatic change to your eating habits, tooth-brushing habits, or paper towel usage, etc., the amount you spend on grocery items should not fluctuate wildly. Therefore, if you're successful with your couponing efforts, then your results should show up vividly as you continue to monitor your monthly grocery spending.

Moderate couponers, especially those who aren't inclined to stockpile discounted items in their homes, should look for a decrease in their average monthly or quarterly grocery expenditure. Extreme couponers, who are more inclined to stockpile goods when the price is right, will be looking for more big-picture results and will be more interested in how much they can save over the course of a year. If you're just getting into couponing and you're choosing to pursue the extreme path, then you'll want to calculate your average monthly expenditure and multiply it by twelve to get your projected yearly expenditure. This is the amount you'd normally spend in a year without couponing. Not to say that the extreme couponer shouldn't also monitor monthly and quarterly expenses; just keep in mind that the bulk purchases, obviously, are going to inflate your spending.

> *Note : If you're a moderate couponer who's still open to the occasional stockpile, then the quarterly expense comparison may be your best tracking option.*

These simple tracking methods can be documented on a regular notepad or on a spreadsheet (see Figure 5).

fig. 5

	Average Monthly		Average Quarterly		Average Yearly	
Marley (An Extreme Couponer)						
	Actual		*Projected (avg. monthly x 3)*		*Projected (avg. monthly x 12)*	
Grocery Spending (Before Coupons)	$ 568.00		$ 1,704.00		$ 6,816.00	
	Actual		*Actual*		*Actual*	
Grocery Spending (After Coupons)	$ 760.00		$ 1,845.00		$ 4,645.00	
George (A Moderate Couponer)						
	Actual		*Projected (avg. monthly x 3)*		*Projected (avg. monthly x 12)*	
Grocery Spending (Before Coupons)	$ 545.00		$ 1,635.00		$ 6,540.00	
	Actual		*Actual*		*Actual*	
Grocery Spending (After Coupons)	$ 470.00		$ 1,355.00		$ 5,381.00	

As is demonstrated in Figure 5, the extreme couponer didn't realize any significant savings until one year into the game, whereas the more moderate couponer saves money right off the bat, but less so in the long run.

You don't have to be an expert in Excel to set up a simple tracking sheet. Just remember to first project out what you'd spend without couponing (based on your known monthly average) and then track what you actually spend after employing the power of couponing.

Gas

Gas for automobiles is another substantial expense that is at once somewhat stable month-by-month *and* subject to significant discounts via promotional offers. Gas promotions are often offered in tandem with credit card purchases or rewards/tracking cards issued by a retailer. Saving money on gas is therefore quite distinct from saving money using regular coupons. The good news is that you don't have to do nearly as much maneuvering. All you have to remember, in most cases, is simply to use the correct card when you're purchasing gas. You may also have to visit a particular brand of gas station in order to qualify for these rewards, but in the grand scheme of things, if you're serious about saving serious money, gas discounts are rightly considered low-hanging fruit.

	Average Monthly		Average Quarterly		Average Yearly	
The Holt Family						
	Actual		*Projected (avg. monthly x 3)*		*Projected (avg. monthly x 12)*	
Gas Expense	$ 205.00		$ 615.00		$ 2,460.00	
	Actual		*Actual*		*Actual*	
Gas Expense (After Using Rewards)	$ 181.00		$ 553.00		$ 2,193.00	

fig. 6 : This figure shows the gas expenses for a fictional family. In most cases, employing gas rewards and rebates will result in a fixed discount off your normal gas expenditure. In the example above, the family is saving about ten percent on gas monthly, quarterly, and yearly.

Restaurants & Entertainment

It's not hard to find coupon offers discounting various restaurant and entertainment expenses. As a result, some couponers may develop a tendency to overspend in this category after they begin saving money with coupons. Doing so is somewhat problematic, as it will not only reduce your bottom-line savings but will also artificially deflate your grocery bill (if you're eating out more, then you're consuming fewer groceries). As a best practice, decide on an appropriate amount that you want to spend monthly on restaurants and entertainment. Stick with this monthly budget for at least a year, then reassess. Remember, it's a well-documented fact that many couponers are inclined to spend *more* money than non-couponers. If you're not careful, overindulging in the great deals at the movie theater and the pizzeria will chip away at your hard-earned progress.

Crowd-sourced coupon offers such as Groupon.com often feature great deals on restaurants. These offers usually feature a coupon that you purchase for a certain amount, let's say twenty-five dollars, that entitles you to thirty-five dollars' worth of food and drinks at a local restaurant. Groupon is also great for other entertainment offerings; just check out the "Things to Do" section on their website and you'll find everything from museums to light plane rides available for a deeply discounted price.

Other Things

The three categories mentioned above are fairly universal, but there are many more types of goods and services subject to the money-saving power of coupons—among them crafts and hobbies, health and fitness, sports and sporting goods, home and hardware, and more. When you're doing your initial assessment of your current budget, be sure to identify and factor in the spending categories relevant to your household. Try to deduce a fair average monthly expenditure amount for each category.

Note : If the category's items or services are only purchased a few times every year, then record the yearly average expense, or the quarterly, whichever you think will be most relevant for tracking purposes.

Simplified Expense Tracking

As mentioned in the previous section, you can record and track your expenses using pen and paper, Excel spreadsheets, or any method of your choosing. If you'd like to work at maximum efficiency, then you can use an automated spending tracker service such as Mint.com, a free personal budgeting service from the makers of TurboTax. The service is cloud-based (you don't have to download anything). It pulls and categorizes spending data out of your bank card and credit card records. You can set budgets for various categories and receive email notifications when you are close to or over any of your budgets. If you make a lot of purchases with cash, you can still use Mint.com, but you'll have to enter your cash purchases manually, just as you would if you were tracking your budgets and spending on a spreadsheet.

Item Recording

Most couponers will do well to start with an even deeper look at their spending habits. ***Item recording*** refers to the tracking of the specific items that you purchase on a weekly or monthly basis. The process is pretty simple. You can use the categories that were established in the previous section and simply list the items that you regularly purchase. You should also add your most-frequented stores to this list for further reference. See Figure 7:

fig. 7

Grocery		Gas	Restaurants + Entertainment	Health + Fitness	
items	venues	venues	venues	items	venues
bread	Kroger	Shell	Papa Johns	Protein powder	Gold's Gym
eggs	Walgreens	BP	Acme Bowling lanes	multi-vitamins	GNC
milk	Hy-Vee		Cinemark Theatre	kettle bells	Onnit.com
tv dinner	CVS		Olive Garden	energy bars	
chicken			Blimpie Subs		

The products you list will form the core of your budget and will ultimately be the products you look for when you're hunting for coupons. Your item recording record should be referred back to from time to time throughout your couponing journey to ensure that you're not letting coupons drive you to make purchases you'd not ordinarily make.

To Recap

- The moderate couponer is more likely to track progress on a monthly or quarterly basis, while the extreme couponer, being more inclined to make mass purchases and stockpile, is better off tracking results on a yearly basis.

- Mint.com can be an invaluable tool for setting budgets and tracking spending.

- "Item Recording" is the process of writing down where you shop and what you buy, so as to prepare yourself for finding the most useful coupons for your shopping preferences.

| 4 |

Coupon Collection & Organization

In This Chapter

- Where to find coupons
- How to organize your coupons
- Buying, selling, and trading coupons
- How to donate expired coupons to US Armed Forces members stationed abroad

Finding Good Coupons

Now that you know exactly who you are (Chapter 1), what you want, and where you shop, it's time to initiate your perpetual search for awesome coupons.

To be most effective you're going to want to cast a wide net, using all available resources, including weekly circulars published in Sunday papers, online coupons, coupons from magazines or publications that you subscribe to, and coupons gifted from or traded with family and friends, online and in person, on websites, on apps, or through social media (Chapter 6). Coupons are everywhere. Just remember that you're looking for deals that correspond to and accommodate your existing shopping habits, and, if you're a more aggressive or extreme couponer, then be prepared to be open-minded about trying a new brand or shopping venue.

In her book, *Extreme Couponing*, Joni Meyer-Crothers emphasizes the importance of coupon quantity. Meyer-Crothers notes how most grocery store items go on sale every eight to twelve weeks and how the key to successful couponing is making sure you always have a coupon ready to help you discount the sale price, thereby ensuring you pay the minimum amount whenever possible for the product, and never regular price.[10]

Let's take a closer look at how to optimally source your coupons.

Collect Coupon Circulars

Circulars, as noted in Chapter 2, are issued by coupon clearinghouses such as Valassis and News America. Circulars can be found as newspaper inserts, usually in the Sunday edition. It is not uncommon for couponers to maintain multiple subscriptions to the newspaper for the sole purpose of obtaining extra copies of the coupon circulars. In the interest of not confusing the delivery man, use a different name for each subscription. Many newspapers offer "Sunday-only" subscriptions, which can save you a little money.

Friends, Family Members, Neighbors, & Networks Are Invaluable

The secret weapon of the effective couponer is her ability to obtain duplicate copies of coupons and use them to purchase multiple units of a deeply discounted item. Getting your hands on duplicate coupons is much easier when you can tap into a network of friends, family members, neighbors, and other couponers. Couponing networks provide trading opportunities and learning opportunities. They can also make the process of couponing more enjoyable from a social perspective.

You'd be surprised at how many people barely even look at the coupons that come with their Sunday papers or come in the mail through circulars. In all likelihood they'll be more than happy to unload some of their "junk mail" on you.

---

[10] Meyer-Crothers, *Extreme Couponing*, 37.

Collect Store Circulars

Store circulars contain store-specific sales information (which is useful in couponing) and may also contain coupons. Although store circulars usually provide store coupons, sometimes the store circulars contain manufacturer coupons, which, if you recall from Chapter 2, can be used anywhere the product is sold. If you stumble across a manufacturer coupon in a store circular then you can easily obtain multiple copies of the coupon by going to the store and grabbing a stack full of their circulars (they will usually have them stacked up somewhere near the front of the store). Remember, you don't have to use a manufacturer coupon at that store; you don't even have to shop at the store if you don't want to. Just get the coupons and go, preferably somewhere that has the item you're interested in on sale.

Make Sure They Know How to Reach You (& What to Send You) at the DMA

If you're not normally receiving coupons by mail, one thing to do is to contact the ***Direct Marketing Association (DMA)*** and make sure you've opted in to the mass mailings that are relevant to you. The DMA sends mass mailings of credit offers, catalogs, magazine offers, banking offers, and of course, coupons.

At the time of this writing, the DMA maintains a subdomain called "DMAChoice.org" where consumers can specify their preferences for the types of mail they wish to receive (and not receive).

Keep Social Tabs

"Follow" and "like" your favorite brands and retailers on social media channels. Keep tabs on these pages to ensure you're aware of any coupons that come down the pipes. See Chapter 7 for more info on finding coupons via social media.

The Internet

In order to fully capitalize on couponing opportunities, you can't ignore the vastness of the Internet. Chapter 6 is devoted entirely to the Internet as a coupon-issuing medium. Couponers can find great deals posted directly on company websites, or they may use one of the hundreds of online deal brokering services.

Mobile

Mobile is definitely the latest and greatest thing in couponing (we'll be covering mobile in more depth in Chapter 7). Companies and third party apps alike regularly issue mobile coupons. When organized on your phone and ready to deploy, mobile coupons can contribute to some very successful shopping trips.

Coupon Clipping Services

There are some companies, such as Klip2save.com, that offer to amass, clip, and mail coupons to you according to your preferences. Coupon clipping services will generally charge you a nominal fee (it's how they remain in business), but if they fit into your overall couponing scheme and routine they can prove well worth the investment.

The Direct Approach

Nothing's stopping you from writing to companies directly and asking that they send you their latest promotional offers. For many companies, the amount of effort it takes to stuff an envelope and send it your way is well worth having someone take a closer look at their offerings.

Guerilla measures

If it suits your personality, you can always go recycle-bin diving for discarded coupon sheets, though I'd recommend doing this in a neighborhood not your own, so no one recognizes you. This stunt was featured on TLC's *Extreme Couponing*, probably for the sake of ratings.

Note : To be clear, going through someone else's trash is not recommended, nor is it legal in some parts of the country.

There are other ways to think outside the box without having to Dumpster dive. For example, you could find businesses that sell Sunday newspapers, like gas stations or coffee shops. Talk to their managers and ask if they'd be willing to give you the coupon inserts from the copies that are discarded at the end of the day. In her book, Meyer-Crothers suggests hitting up assisted living homes and nursing homes, since many of the residents receive the newspaper but don't need any of the coupons because their meals are provided in the facility.[11]

Don't Be Afraid of Couponer's Vernacular

"Vernacular" refers to a localized way of speaking, a local dialect if you will. If you make the wise choice to get engaged in the online couponing community, you'll be quick to notice the couponer's vernacular. You may have heard of terms like **BOGO** (buy one get one free), but if you're just beginning, you probably don't have any idea what is meant by "**SS**" or "**Catalina**." Don't worry, after a few months of coupon immersion you'll pick up the language. If you'd like to jump right in, then have a look through the Glossary of Terms at the back of this book.

---

[11] Meyer-Crothers, *Extreme Couponing*, 44.

Coupon Organization Methods

Now we're going to look at a few approaches to basic coupon organization. This step is best explored after you've accumulated a sizeable stash of coupons.

Gather your coupons together in a single file folder or portable organizer. While organizing your collected coupons in a single file, sort through the coupons to check for the products that match the items and the venues you specified in your item recording process and mark them with a yellow highlighter pen. Don't hesitate to discard the coupons you know you won't use, or file them in a separate "trading folder" to trade with others.

The way you organize your coupons will depend on your personal preference and shopping style. The most common methods of organization involve clipping coupons into a folder or file organizer alphabetized by name or category of product, but any kind of sorting may be used, such as sorting by expiration date or sorting by store isle. The idea is to have all of your coupons centrally located and organized so that you don't have to search for the coupons you need when you are in the store. Smaller pocket organizers may come in handy instead of carrying around a folder or binder. Whatever method you use, make sure that it's appropriate for your *couponing type*—as defined in Chapter 1— and that you are comfortable with the system. At this point in your setup process you should take your time. It might take several hours to set up a system that will best accommodate you. If you plan on couponing for any significant length of time, then you will fare a lot better with a well-designed system. Some specific examples of coupon organization methods include the following:

1. The Binder Method

The coupon binder is a three-ring binder with plastic, segmented pages to file coupons. With this method, you can page through all of your collected coupons and visibly see what coupons you have available. The binder method offers a portable solution, which is highly recommended. When you visit a store, any store, you will always bring your coupon binder with you. That way, if there are any sale items that you weren't aware of, you'll be ready to put your coupons to use.

2. *The Hybrid Method*

The hybrid method, like the binder method, involves keeping your coupons in a binder organized by date. Depending on the volume of coupons you're working with, you can delineate the sections of your binder according to the week or according to the month (or both). At the front of each binder section, use baseball card holders to store the coupons that you've cut out and are sure you're going to use. Behind the baseball card holders in each section insert the standard plastic sleeves and use them to store full coupon circulars that you can reference as needed.

To ensure your coupon book doesn't become bogged down by expired coupons, you can use a tool called the Sunday Coupon Preview (available at http://www.sundaycouponpreview.com/) which will list all of the coupons included in a given circular along with their expiration dates. Print this list and circle or highlight the forward-most coupon expiration date (the expiration date furthest away from the current date). This way, you can easily thumb through your binder and eliminate coupons and whole circulars that contain only expired coupons.[12]

Note : Using the Sunday Coupon Preview can help you stay organized while using several of the methods featured in this section, not just the Hybrid Method.

---

[12] http://gooddealmama.com/free-it-forward-donate-expired-coupons-to-the-military/

3. The File Box

This method is better for long-term coupon strategies for collecting coupons three months (or longer) out. You can organize coupons within the labeled file folders by date and type, or whatever other method you desire.

4. The Scrapbook Album

Using a scrapbook organizer, you can save individual coupons or entire inserts, similar to the hybrid method. Also, you can add organization tabs for specific coupon types or for organizing coupons by store.

5. The Mega Coupon Bag

This coupon bag is often sold online and looks like a small backpack or purse; it often includes a file folder and other organizational pockets for couponing purposes.

6. The Day Planner

This is a small day planner repurposed for couponing. You can carry a small pencil or pen to make notes, organize coupons under different tabs, and store loose coupons in a clear plastic organizer.

7. The Couponizer

The Couponizer is an 8" x 5-1/4" booklet with eighteen grocery coupon pockets, four non-grocery coupon pockets, and three gift card and shopper loyalty card sleeves. It also includes a twenty-page tear-off shopping list paper pad, a "coupstacker" pre-sorting mat color-coded to match system pockets, a "couptracker" fifteen-page spiral bound list pad with cardboard backing, scissors, and a clear vinyl zippered carrying bag.

8. The App Folder

With most coupons and rebates being done digitally these days, it may help to create a folder on your phone or tablet specifically for couponing/savings apps. This alone would be a huge time-saver so you wouldn't have to scroll through page after page to find all your savings apps.

Tip : Save some space in your binder, notebook, planner, etc., for a copy of the coupon policies from each store you frequent. Knowing store policy will help you navigate complicated situations and will allow you take advantage of double coupons whenever possible.

Which coupon organizational system is best?

We spent a while trying to get together a good answer for this question, only to come to the boring old conclusion that different systems work for different couponers, with different objectives, and different shopping habits. The frugal/extreme couponer, for instance, may use two methods: a hybrid binder so she's prepared for on-the-spot deals, as well as a file box for preparing high volume purchases. A fun/moderate couponer may get a kick out of the Couponizer and find that it does the job perfectly as far they're concerned. Even couponing expert Joni Meyer-Crothers can't definitely recommend one system over another.

Seriously, do whatever feels right for you. A lot of people will try one way and find it doesn't work for them, so they'll try something else. Take the time to work through and see what system works best for you.[13]

Buying, Selling, & Trading Coupons

Most coupons have a disclaimer printed on them that reads: "Coupon may be void if copied, transferred, reproduced, sold, or exchanged." If you are worried about getting into legal trouble while buying, selling, or trading coupons, don't worry.

---

[13] Meyer-Crothers, *Extreme Couponing*, 101.

This disclaimer is printed on coupons in order to protect the manufacturer in a situation where the coupon is being used in a fraudulent manner, in which case the manufacturer needs to void the coupon permanently. What the manufacturer is trying to prevent is the illegal duplication and distribution of coupons. Coupons are serialized, meaning there is a unique number printed on each copy of any given coupon to prevent unauthorized duplication. So, as long as you aren't photocopying coupons and trying to use, sell, or trade the copies, you aren't violating any laws. However, always make sure to check for any specific coupon policies, either printed on the physical coupon or mentioned elsewhere, such as in a store publication or website, or even on a manufacturer's website.

Trading with your fellow couponers can be a lot of fun and can do a lot to help you stock up on the coupons most relevant to your shopping needs. In addition to trading in social communities, online, at church, with other members of the PTA, etc., you can also find (or set up) coupon trading posts. This is commonly done at community centers or public libraries and involves the use of a designated coupon bank that you can make deposits into and withdrawals from. If you're in charge of setting up the box, make sure you institute some common-sense guidelines for proper maintenance. That is, make sure people are aware that they're expected to contribute (deposit), not just take coupons whenever they please. And make sure that a system is in place to minimize the presence of expired coupons. If you like, you can even use an accordion file or some other segregation tool to divvy up the coupons by category.

If you're not very social or can't imagine how you'd ever find a "couponing club" to be a part of, don't underestimate the power of even just one or two friends with whom you can trade and bounce ideas off of. A small social network is better than no social network. Furthermore, no matter where you live, you'll always be able to connect with couponing communities online. The discussion forum FatWallet. com offers a fruitful haven for deal seekers of all stripes, including couponers. Set up an account and have a poke around. It couldn't hurt.

What to Do with Expired Coupons

Expired coupons (manufacturer coupons, not store coupons) can be donated to US troops deployed abroad. US troops deployed abroad may use manufacturer coupons six months after they've expired. The most requested coupon type for soldiers overseas is food/grocery. The second most requested coupon type is baby supplies. You can find more information about donating expired coupons at https://www. couponcabin.com/troops/.

To Recap

- Quantity is key when it comes to obtaining coupons; get as many as you can and trade the ones you don't need.

- There are several organizational systems that can make couponing easier; find the one that works best for you.

- Coupons are serialized and you're free to use as many of them as you like, as long as you don't photocopy the coupon or violate store policy.

- Trading coupons can be fun and worthwhile, and the Internet offers couponers a chance to participate in vibrant trading and tip-sharing.

- If your coupons are less than six months past their expiration date, they can be sent to and used by US troops stationed overseas.

| 5 |

Use Coupons to Save Thousands

In This Chapter

- Choosing a shopping method for grocery couponing
- Understanding the "one coupon per purchase" rule
- How to get great deals by using coupons to purchase items already on sale
- Using "coupon stacking" to combine manufacturer discounts with store discounts
- Why double couponing has fallen out of favor with retailers
- How to stock up on items that you can get for extraordinary prices
- How to tell whether a coupon is highly valuable or a waste of time

While there are numerous coupons for discounts, rebates, and rewards for a wide range of products, grocery coupons remain the most popular and widely used form of coupon. Grocery coupons offer the maximum savings and rewards for your couponing efforts. Just as there are different strategies for couponing based on shopping habits and preferences, there are different ways of approaching grocery couponing. The easiest of these methods is casual grocery couponing, where coupons may be collected while reading a Sunday paper or other periodical. This "coupon shopping" method is a good way to compile a grocery list based on what coupons are available. Just make sure you resist the impulse to purchase an item you don't need simply because there's a coupon for it.

Another shopping method is "meal planning," where a weekly schedule is drafted with specific foods for breakfast, lunch, and dinner on specific days of the week, and then a shopping list is compiled of items needed for that week's menu, along with applicable coupons. Your weekly meal planning will drive your grocery shopping strategy and hence your couponing strategy.

Regardless of how you initiate your shopping trip, you should brace yourself for a difficult first outing as a couponer. Shopping while rigorously using coupons is a much different experience than normal shopping. It follows a different rhythm. For example, when you're a couponer, you always take out your coupon and set it aside immediately after you take the item off the shelf and place it in your cart. You don't do what normal shoppers do, which is wait until they're in the checkout line before taking out the coupons they're going to use. Think about it—on most shopping trips you're not going to be working with only one or two coupons. It's going to be more like twenty or thirty. You may even find it useful to carry a small roll of scotch tape with you when you shop and affix each coupon to its product before you place it in the cart.

When you first begin, be sure to give yourself plenty of time for your shopping outings. You may find that your original organizational scheme has a few defects and needs some modifications. This is normal and expected.

What Is Really Meant by "One Coupon Per Purchase"

Throughout this book we've been talking about ways in which you can acquire, purchase, or trade your way to multiple copies of the same coupon. If you're looking to maximize value, whether as an "extreme" or a "moderate" couponer, then it's imperative that you understand what is meant (and what is not meant) by the "one coupon per purchase" disclaimer that appears in the fine print of many manufacturer coupons.

A huge mistake that is made by many would-be couponers is assuming that "one coupon per purchase," or some equivalent of that phrasing, means that each customer is entitled to purchase only one of the item or group of items using one coupon. I still remember going to the grocery store as a child with my thrifty and slightly eccentric father. He would send me, armed with a coupon and its corresponding product, to a separate checkout aisle in what he presumed to be a clever work-around of the "one coupon per purchase" restriction. Throughout my life, I'd never thought to question his rationale, until I began to study the art of couponing.

The "one coupon per purchase" restriction simply means that you must present one valid coupon for each product (or specified grouping of products, like *buy 2 get 1 free*, etc.) that you purchase. That is, you can't use three copies of a fifty-cents-off coupon to get $1.50 off a given product. This is where all the effort you spent accumulating multiple copies of coupons pays off. Remember what we learned in Chapter 2: the manufacturer (the clearinghouse, technically) is ultimately going to reimburse the grocery store for the entire value of every valid coupon it collects. The grocery store has no reason to care how many manufacturer coupons are used by any given customer. In this way valid coupons operate as another form of currency, and, for the grocers, each purchase is just another sale.

On the other hand, some stores do limit the number of coupons you can use for the same item. They see the use of multiple coupons as problematic in that they don't want one or two customers emptying an entire shelf of product. Stores which limit multiple coupons may not be the best choices for extreme couponers but may still be viable for more casual couponing types.

Special thanks to KrazyCouponLady.com for compiling a list of phrasings commonly used to describe the "one coupon per purchase" restriction:[14]

- Limit one coupon per item purchased.
- Limit one coupon per purchase of specified item(s).
- Limit one coupon per purchase of product specified.
- Only one coupon is redeemable per purchase and only on specified products and sizes.

Matching Sales to Coupons – The Eclipse of Value

One of the most exciting and visceral pay-offs of couponing is finding that perfect eclipse of a solid sale price and a solid coupon. When these two factors converge around a product that you like (especially a nonperishable one that you can stock up on), that's when the real magic happens. Matching the sale to the coupon, for most couponers, is where the rubber meets the road.

The routine goes a little something like this: you receive your weekly grocery store circulars in the mail, you scan through them and mark the items that you're interested in, then you cross-check the sale items with your organized coupon collection, looking for matches. Conventional wisdom holds that items go on sale every eight to twelve weeks.

> *Note : Remember, grocery store circulars are not the same as coupon circulars. Check the glossary of terms in the back of this book if you are still unclear on the difference.*

Using Automated Deal-Matching Services

In this book's introduction, contributing author Simon Basamanowicz described his foray into the world of automated deal-matching, a service that automatically tracks weekly sale

---

[14] "What does 'One Coupon Per Purchase' mean?" *The Krazy Coupon Lady*. (February 10, 2010): accessed June 1, 2016.

prices and matches them to manufacturer coupons currently in circulation. In the intro, www.grocerycouponnetwork.com was mentioned as a service provider of this nature. There are countless other blogs and websites that now offer sale-to-coupon matching and several other services to boot. You should have little trouble finding one or several online resources that fit your shopping habits as well as your couponing "type." Several of these resources offer convenient shopping list creation services, whereby you can print out your shopping list and expediently incorporate your coupons. Many couponing blogs and sites will also direct you to printable coupons or coupon clipping services that are coordinated to match the regional sales in your area.

Stacking Up Extra Savings

Stacking, in couponer's vernacular, is a term used to describe using two coupons to discount one product. This is almost always accomplished by using both a store-issued coupon and a manufacturer coupon. Two manufacturer coupons generally cannot be stacked together, nor can two store-issued coupons.

Author of *Extreme Couponing* Joni Meyer-Crothers reports that Walgreens and Target are the two retailers most likely to have awesome offers available thanks to coupon matching.[15] This is likely the result of these two retailers' tendency for issuing their own coupons. Grocery stores, in my experience, don't issue store coupons quite as frequently as big-chain drug stores like Walgreens, or superstores like Target. But many of them offer something even better—double-coupon days!

Taking It to the Next Level with Double Couponing

This term refers to a particular type of grocery store promotion, usually offered on certain days of the week or once a month. The

---

[15] Meyer-Crothers, *Extreme Couponing*, 114.

grocery store makes the determination of when to offer the promotion. Double couponing allows customers to receive twice the value of their coupons. If I have a coupon that promises twenty-five cents off a jar of pickles, then I'll receive a total of fifty cents off on double-coupon day. When double-couponing promotions are run by grocers, the manufacturers still only reimburse the store for the stated value of the coupon. The second half of the discount is eaten by the grocery store.

There are usually specific rules associated with double couponing that will vary from store to store and region to region, so be sure to get familiar with those rules before you use this technique. For example, some grocery stores will not allow you to double up coupons more valuable than fifty cents, a fairly common restriction. In order to make prudent decisions about where to use your coupons, it's important that you familiarize yourself with the coupon policies of all the retailers you frequent. As was mentioned in Chapter 3, we recommend printing out the coupon policies of your go-to retailers and keeping them filed in your couponing notebook for quick reference.

As has been noted previously in this book, grocery stores are heavily regionalized, in terms of both pricing and policy. Some corporate grocery companies even maintain a multitude of different DBA (doing business as) names across the country. For example, the Kroger Company, the largest supermarket chain on earth as of 2015, maintains a multitude of DBA names, such as Gerbes in the Midwest, Ralph's in Southern California, Smith's in the "mountain states" of Utah and Wyoming, and many more.

Because of the heavy regionalization, the Internet may not always have on-point and accurate information about your local grocery store's policies with regard to couponing. As a best practice, don't rely on the Internet but contact your favorite grocers by phone to get the final word on double couponing. Double couponing can save you a lot of money if you leverage it well. It's worth noting, however, that the practice has fallen out of favor in recent years thanks to the popularity of extreme couponing. After the wave of hype surrounding the TLC television series, some stores, tired of their shelves being stripped bare by savvy couponers, discontinued double-coupon days altogether.[16] Though this may sound like a serious blow to the couponing community, it's really not so bad. Even if you don't make double couponing a part of your shopping routine, you still stand to realize tremendous overall savings through the matching of coupons to store sales. Furthermore, if you make matching your primary focus, then you'll have more shopping days to choose from, as most sales last for about a week. If you get too hung up on double-coupon days, then you're forced into shopping on one specific day alongside a swarm of other deal-hungry shoppers.

Stockpiling

The core of your grocery couponing strategy should begin with a detailed budget (Chapter 3) and/or meal plan. This approach is always better than allowing the specific deals and coupons for a certain week to guide your shopping decisions. With that said, the *stockpiling* technique is useful for maximizing your budget potential by stocking up on whatever coupons are available for a limited time *or* during a specific sale cycle. For example, couponers love to brag about how they never pay for basic household items like shampoo and toothpaste. If you have a coupon that will get you a dollar off a three-dollar tube of toothpaste (two dollars off during a double-coupon day) and that coupon expires at the end of the week, then you should go ahead and use as many copies of the coupon as you have, to stock up on toothpaste. Now, let's say the coupon doesn't expire for another few weeks, *but* there's a sale on the toothpaste, bringing the price down from three

---

[16] Brad Tuttle, "The War Against Couponers: Double Coupons Going Way of the Dinosaur," *Time* (April 2012): http://business.time.com/2012/04/03/the-war-against-couponers-double-coupons-going-way-of-the-dinosaur/

dollars to two. Again, you'd want to capitalize on the opportunity to purchase the item at a discount and add the toothpaste to your stock at home.

If you're on a tight week-by-week or month-by-month budget, then don't get discouraged if you have to pass up a deal or two. There will always be more. If you have more flexibility in your budget, then keep in mind that taking advantage of deals on stockpile-able nonperishable items (like toothpaste), when they're available, will cut down the expense of future shopping trips.

Stockpiling vs. Hoarding : The 80/20 Principle

The difference between reasonable stockpiling associated with couponing and compulsive hoarding should be clarified: stockpiling is a strategy for saving money in the long term by acquiring eminently usable goods, while hoarding is more often associated with the compulsive collection of goods that aren't necessarily useable within any reasonable time frame. One way to vividly explore this distinction and to ensure that couponing doesn't become a gateway to hoarding is to perform an 80/20 analysis of your grocery pantry. The 80/20 principle is credited to a management theorist named Joseph M. Juran. It says that in any system 80 percent of the assets will be used 20 percent of the time. In terms of what grocery items are in your kitchen pantry, the principle would assert that 20 percent of the items are used 80 percent of the time, while 80 percent of the items are used 20 percent of the time. In other words, you have items that are your go-to items, those you're comfortable cooking with, that you replenish often, and that you enjoy eating. In my house, these items would be peanut butter, cereal, milk, bread, and eggs, to name a few. My 80 percent might include canned beans, instant mashed potatoes, and the frozen pork shoulder in my freezer that's been there for four months. Now, to ensure that you remain an efficient couponer and never cross over into hoarder territory, it's essential that you avoid using coupons to overstock your 80 percent. What tends to happen in these households is that the 80 percent soon becomes 85 percent, then 90 percent, and so forth. Just because I have a freezer full of pork shoulder that I bought at a great price doesn't necessarily mean I will (or should) change my eating habits to favor an abundance of pork shoulder. All it really means is that I now have less space in my freezer. Remember, couponing should complement your shopping habits, not inform them.

Preordering – An Exercise in Couponing Diplomacy

If you've been successful in accumulating multiple copies of a useful coupon and plan on making a potentially shelf-clearing purchase when auspicious sale conditions present themselves, then consider preordering the product. Preordering involves contacting the grocery store and informing the manager of your intent to make a bulk purchase using coupons during an upcoming or current sale. Preordering will ensure that you have the quantity available to purchase and will also help the store avoid running out of the product.

Don't underestimate the importance of using tactics like preordering and other communicative measures to establish a good relationship with the powers that be at your local grocery stores and other retailers. As we've frequently mentioned throughout this chapter, grocery stores operate with a high degree of regional autonomy. Formal corporate policies will often grant managers the authority to limit coupon usage by the customer. Take, for instance, the corporate policy of Wal-Mart containing the following dictates with regard to couponing:

- We have the ability to limit the number of identical coupons and the number of coupons for the same item per transaction.

- If coupon value exceeds the price of the item, the excess may be given to the customer as cash or applied toward the basket purchase.

- In all situations, we reserve the right to limit purchase quantities to typical retail purchase quantities or one-per-customer or household and to exclude dealers.[17]

You shouldn't get discouraged when you read policies like Wal-Mart's. Just because they reserve the right to limit your coupon usage doesn't meant that they will (or that they *should* from a business perspective). If you think about it, it's usually not good business to limit sales of items (except perhaps on double-coupon days, when the store is eating half of the discount). Manufacturer coupons will ultimately be reimbursed, regardless of how many identical coupons are used by the customer at any given time. If you're courteous and communicative, then store decision makers should eventually come around to the reality that your business, just like any other business, is helping their store. Just do all you can to be aware of and accommodate any concerns they may have, such as the clearing off of their shelves. Store managers may also look unfavorably on the prospect of processing one hundred coupons at checkout time. You can offset this concern by making arrangements to shop at non-peak hours and informing the cashier and the manager, when possible, when you're coming through with your ready-to-stockpile collection of couponing plunder.

Avoiding Bad Coupons

Remember, couponing is marketing, and marketing is an attempt to convince you to buy something that you may not have otherwise

---

[17] "Coupon Policy," *Walmart Policies and Guidelines*, http://corporate.walmart.com/policies: accessed June 1, 2016.

considered. We can even take a lesson here from the first coupon—the coupon for the free Coca-Cola described in Chapter 2. The Coca-Cola coupon was issued in 1888, just two years after the launch of the Coca-Cola Company. The vast majority of Americans had never tried any kind of soda pop. Why should they? Coca-Cola's answer was, because it's free with a coupon.

Coupons often feature discounts on random, nonessential items such as Tupperware containers, Mio water-enhancers, and new soft drinks offering no nutritional value whatsoever. Issuing coupons is a great way for a manufacturer to try to create a market where none currently exists. Couponers who are motivated by frugality should strive to avoid being a marketing guinea pig, even if they can do so cheaply. If you don't have any pressing need for a product, if you don't normally use a product, or if you can get a generic product or another brand for less (even after the coupon discount), then there's no need to use the coupon. Throw it away.

Speaking of name brands, it can be quite frustrating for the frugal-minded couponer, primarily interested in saving money, to come across scores of coupons offering very modest discounts on name brands. If only these coupons came with a price listing alongside their house brand equivalent, then it would be immediately apparent whether the coupon was worth saving.

What About Brand Loyalty?

Here's the ultimate question: if I have a coupon that saves me a dollar off a name brand but it's still more expensive than the house brand or generic, then do I really save money? The answer to the question, of course, depends on the type of couponer I am, and with specific regard to my sense of brand loyalty. If I have a strong preference for the brand being discounted, then I should certainly buy, and in large quantities. If I'm dead set on saving as much money as possible, then I should throw the coupon away and purchase the house brand.

Using Coupons to Bust Routines

In some situations a coupon may present an opportunity to try out a new type of grocery item or a new brand at a highly competitive price. In these situations, couponers may get more money-saving mileage out of their coupons if they're willing to try something new. In this way, the couponer can stay effective by going with the flow of the marketing effort, as opposed to struggling against it.

Illegal Coupons

In the Internet age, illegal and counterfeit coupons have become more prevalent than ever before. An interest group known as the **Coupon Information Corporation (CIC)** keeps a database of known fraudulent coupons. The database can be accessed at www.couponinformationcenter.com/.

When you encounter a coupon that's suspect, either online or in printed form, a little common sense can go a long way. Your first hint is going to be the overall quality of the design and, if it's an online coupon, the look and feel of the issuing website, as well as any published feedback from the website's users. Coupons that appear to be photocopied are never a good bet. Also, if the offer proposed seems outlandish or too good to be true, then you may have a fraudulent coupon on your hands. Fake coupons often promise totally free products that ordinarily would never be free. They may also be issued without expiration dates. A good rule of thumb is to be highly skeptical if you're being asked to pay money to receive "amazing" coupons. The legitimate coupon clipping services, such as Klip2Save.com, aren't offering coupons that you "can't get anywhere else." If you're in doubt, always check the CIC database.

How to Recognize the Coupons That Are Truly Valuable

My father had this uncanny gift when it came to sales and coupons. Being a business major and a finance professional, he was quite good with numbers. When he spotted a grocery item priced favorably (thanks to a coupon, a sale, or both) his inner thriftiness would kick into high gear and he'd start loading up on the item hurriedly as if he were afraid that at any moment another shopper would awaken to the amazing deal at hand and start to horn in on his action.

Unlike my father, I'm unfortunately not always able to make rapid judgments about whether an offer at a given price at a given quantity is a good deal. I'm more prone to require a few moments to think over a proposed price and take my time deciding whether or not it fits into my overall shopping plan. I would imagine that there are more out there like me who could use some help in determining how to spot valuable coupons and deals in general. As was mentioned in Chapter 1, however, couponing is first and foremost an art and not a science. The best tips, therefore, are highly situational in nature:

- Is the coupon discounting a product that appears on your Item Record (Chapter 3), that is, a product that you normally buy? If not, does the coupon *actively replace* a purchase that you'd otherwise make? For example, if you're a frequent consumer of peanut butter but have a coupon that allows you to purchase a similar quantity of almond butter at a lower price, then your almond butter coupon will actively replace your standard peanut butter purchase.

- Does the coupon have an expiration date longer than three months? Remember, items go on sale every eight to twelve weeks. If you find a coupon for a product that you buy that's going to stay valid for at least twelve weeks, then you'll likely be able to catch that product on sale at some point. Find copies of that coupon and stock up come sale time!

• Does the coupon discount a name-brand product to a price lower than that of the house brand or generic equivalent? Unless you've got a hankering for Kroger brand vegetable oil, then use your coupon to buy the name brand and save some money!

More Opportunities for Grocery Savings with Coupons

One of the nice things about becoming a great couponer is that, over time, you become "coupon vigilant," meaning that you get better and more efficient with your filing systems, you instinctively scan through the supermarket circulars for that elusive manufacturer coupon or whole-purchase coupon. Whole-purchase coupons discount the entirety of a single purchase, usually after you've spent a certain amount. An example would be "Save $5 off your purchase of $50 or more." For the well-practiced couponer, offers like these never go to waste, especially not at the grocery store. As soon as they set foot in the store, they pick up the latest store circular (unless they brought their own) and do a quick scan to search for coupons. Any whole-purchase coupons are quickly cut and added to the top of the coupon que and will help the couponer pile on the savings come checkout time.

Rebates and rewards are other forms of savings that you can factor into your grocery shopping strategy. If you consider the dollar value of coupon rebates, the long-term saving potential is readily apparent and even exciting. Similarly, rewards based on shopping habits and spending quantity (rewards-based coupons) can provide not only discounts but free items and other shopping perks as well. When you receive your extra coupons at checkout with your receipt, your trusty couponer's notebook allows you to promptly file them away in the appropriate section, where you're certain not to forget them if there's a chance to put them to good use.

If you don't receive your favorite stores' ad flyers along with your local newspaper, then always be sure to pick them up at the store and peruse them before you shop. You will often find coupons or rebates in the flyer that aren't well-advertised. Sometimes the value of these in-house flyer coupons is quite substantial: *"Free carton of eggs with a purchase over $25."* Who isn't going to buy eggs? And, moreover, who isn't going to spend more than twenty-five dollars at the grocery store?

Accessing a store's website will also often reveal their current sales for the week. Several grocer websites will allow users to create and print shopping lists and may even allow them to add coupons to their store cards.

One of the most popular recent coupon and rebate campaigns has been grocery chains partnering with gas stations. These deals, usually called "fuel perks" or some variation thereof, give participants rebates on gas at specific companies. You buy items with the "fuel perks" logo and you receive points to enjoy gas discounts. Some thrifty customers can earn up to thirty cents off per gallon at participating gas stations. I don't think I need to tell you how incredibly helpful that could be! Other grocery stores don't even bother labeling their "fuel perk" items, but simply give you a fixed amount of gas reward points based on the amount you spend. For the experienced couponer, taking advantage of these auxiliary savings opportunities is a cake walk, as long as you're diligent and creative in the upkeep of your organizational system. For instance, if your "fuel perks" only work at certain gas stations, try using a location-based alarm on your smartphone to remind you when you're in close proximity to the preferred gas station.

Using a multi-tier couponing strategy that includes clipped coupons, reward cards, Internet (Chapter 6) and mobile coupons (Chapter 7), along with smart planning, will provide many different options for savings on grocery bills and beyond.

One way in which you can combine resources and maximize your overall savings is to first compile as many regular printed coupons as you can, see what items on your shopping list are covered, and then look online for coupons for the items that are left over or for the items that are currently on sale. Don't get frustrated if you can't locate a coupon for a particular item. In many cases there is significant overlap between the items that are discounted via print coupons and the items discounted via online coupons. Spend a fixed amount of time searching for each coupon, no more than five to ten minutes, and move on to your next search.

You should also check out all the great ways companies lure customers in by offering rebates and coupons just for signing up for their newsletter. Large chains like Michael's craft store will send newsletter subscriber coupons, printable or mobile, for upwards of 40 percent off an entire purchase. Once you sign up and start receiving the newsletter, these coupons come very often. Michael's is certainly not the only store that follows this practice, and you'd be amazed at what you can actually save when you "befriend" your favorite retailers through newsletter subscriptions or on social media (Chapter 7).

One final way to find the best coupons and savings is by checking your receipt. Most stores offer cash back or savings on your next purchase of things you just bought on this shopping trip. Also, many retailers offer sweepstakes entries or money off of your next shopping trip for answering short surveys. When you take advantage of savings opportunities on many different fronts, the dollars begin to stack up.

To Recap

- Grocery shopping is the central arena of couponing; if you know how to work the system you can save thousands of dollars on a regular basis.

- Good grocery couponing involves a combination of tactics: accumulate useful coupons, wait for items to go on sale, buy in bulk.

- Grocery stores operate with a substantial degree of regional authority, especially when it comes to their policies on couponing; be courteous and communicative when making large-scale purchases from a grocer, or they may shut you down.

- "Bad coupons" may be those that offer no competitive price advantage over their house brand or generic equivalents, those that push a product without an established market, or those that are fraudulent in origin.

- If your goal as a couponer is to be frugal, then a good coupon will either help you get a low price on an item you regularly purchase or an equivalent item that preempts the necessity of the item you regularly purchase.

| 6 |

The Internet Changed Couponing

In This Chapter

- How the right websites can help you step up your couponing game
- The three most important benefits of online couponing
- A profile of six different couponing websites, and how to separate the good from the bad

Up to this point in our couponing adventure, we've been fairly old school with regard to strategy. And the old school strategy isn't complicated. In fact, it can be described in one sentence: collect coupons, match with sales, purchase in bulk, stockpile, repeat. The advent of online couponing and online specialty sites devoted to assisting couponers has essentially created a way for shoppers to outsource much of the organizational work inherent to couponing. But a quick look at the top couponing websites, such as TheKrazyCouponLady.com or Coupons. com, can turn off a lot of would-be online couponers. The sites look too noisy and complex. The irony is that these sites, the noisy and complex-looking ones, can be incredibly helpful if you learn how to use them. They have to throw out a lot of information up front, because not all shoppers are alike and there are universes within universes of coupons out there, for groceries alone. It's enough to make your head spin.

One of the best ways to take advantage of coupons and other related deals is to find high-quality online websites with tools designed to accommodate your couponing efforts. These tools include print-on-demand coupons, social media promotions, rebates, regional sales listings, deal-matching guides, and mobile applications, all of which are sure to add considerable value to your overall financial savings. The added beauty of learning to coupon online is that you stand to save a fair amount of time, time that you'd otherwise spend fumbling through ads and coupon sheets and working the scissors. In this chapter we're going to look at ways in which couponing websites function to make couponing more efficient and effective for shoppers like you.

What Are the Main Benefits of Online Couponing?

One of the many ways in which online and mobile coupons have changed the game is by their sheer convenience. With a little bit of tech savviness, even the busiest person can utilize coupons without having to spend the time hunting for and clipping traditional paper coupons. Not only do these tools expedite coupon delivery (straight from the Internet to your computer or phone), they can also be leveraged to promote better coupon organization, budgeting, and shopping strategies.

Website and mobile application couponing tools are sometimes tied in to other new trends involving social media like Facebook, Twitter, Pinterest, and Google+. Even if your computer skills are lacking, most of these digital tools are so easy to learn and use that you may find yourself using them more than you think.

There are three primary advantages that the Internet has brought to the world of couponing. Understanding these principal advantages will provide you with a systematic way to evaluate whether a given couponing website (and there are hundreds of them) will turn out to be particularly useful to you.

1. The Internet Allows Coupons to Proliferate

Before the Internet, hard-core couponers were stuck running around collecting newspaper inserts. Perhaps the more aggressive among them would send out letters to manufacturers requesting promotional packs in the mail. The Internet has provided a way for manufacturers, stores, and entrepreneurs to provide coupons to the public.

The ability to use a search engine to find and immediately print the coupons you're interested in has also added a layer of convenience and expediency. Couponers now have more opportunities to customize their coupon collections in a way that best complements their shopping habits. They can stock up when they're preparing for a big purchase or they can sell their coupons to web-based distributors and middlemen who make their living on the floors of virtual coupon trading posts.

2. Internet-Based Service Providers Can Take The Leg Work Out of Deal-Matching

One of the ways in which various couponing websites establish loyal followings is by offering deal-matching data, whereby coupons in circulation can be paired with regional sale prices to procure an exceptionally deep discount. Sites like the now defunct Grocery Game monetized this service by requiring users to sign up for a monthly recurring billable subscription. Other sites make their revenue by offering the deal-matching service for free and then selling ad space on their site, building up their newsletter subscriber base, and participating in cross-promotions with retailers and manufacturers.

Furthermore, many couponing websites will not only show you where to find the best deal match-ups, they will also direct you to a site where you can print the required coupons. The dynamic of deal-matching is thus completely changed. Before, the standard process involved first accumulating coupons and then carefully organizing them in such a way that they could be easily referred to when the sale prices came around every eight to twelve weeks. Online couponing, by contrast, gives shoppers the ability to rapidly scan sale prices and immediately procure corresponding coupons (see Figure 8).

Product	Sale Price	Coupon	Final Price
Crest Toothpaste 5.8-6.2 oz	$ 3.50	Crest Toothpaste, 3 oz or more Liquid Gel or Kids Toothpaste, any EXCLUDING trial/travel size, .25/1 (06-25-26) PG-5/29	$ 3.25
Crest Toothpaste 5.8-6.2 oz	$ 3.50	Crest Toothpaste, 3 oz or larger or Liquid Gel, any EXCLUDING Cavity, Baking Soda, Tartar Control and Kids .50/1 (active) Group A-05/01 Print it Twice	$ 3.00
Dove Bar Soap 2 Pack	$ 3.99		$ 3.99
L'Oreal Shampoo or Conditioner 8.5 oz	$ 6.49	L'Oreal Paris Product, any $1/1 (active) This Link-07/19	$ 5.49
Oral-B Glide Floss 43.7-54.7 yards or Floss Picks 30-75 ct.	$ 3.50	Oral B Glide Floss 35M or larger, or Oral B Glide Floss Picks 30 ct or higher, any EXCLUDING trial/travel size, $1/1 (06-25-26) PG-5/29	$ 2.50

fig. 8 : The chart section above was copied from a website called GrocerySmarts.com (discussed later in this chapter)

Figure 8 shows a sample listing of simplified content that was pulled from a weekly store circular and posted for free online. Note how the links to various coupons are available for instant access within the chart. Pretty amazing.

3. Couponing Trading & Tip Networks Are Now Limitless in Scale

You now have a lot more people with whom you can trade coupons and share advice. Many couponing websites and blogs are congregating grounds for vibrant communities of couponers. Certain websites offer incentives for participants to upload new coupons to the site to share with others. In this way, social networks are apt to transform into vast coupon libraries in which you can find all the coupons you need for your shopping endeavors.

How to Choose the Best Online Resources

Depending on your couponing *type* (Chapter 1) and what you value in the way of couponing and online deals, you may end up with any combination of couponing websites as your go-to favorites. Rather than attempting to tell you where to shop, we decided it would be a better use of time to look through a few of the more popular or noteworthy websites out there and suggest some ways by which you might evaluate their usefulness to your couponing objectives. Though this chapter will focus primarily on traditional websites, Chapter 7 will extend our analysis into the territory of social media and apps.

Some notable coupon web sites include the following:

1. CouponMom.com

CouponMom.com is the web-based center of operations for Stephanie Nelson. Nelson has spent nearly two decades mastering the art of couponing and showing others the way. Her methods have been featured on the *Today* show, *Oprah*, and *Dr. Oz*, where she often harkens back to the same general themes. She believes that drug stores such as CVS and Walgreens are some of the best venues for couponing, particularly when it comes to coupling good coupon offers with store-brand over-the-counter pharmacy products, such as cold medicine. She also emphasizes the importance of saving your coupons until the items you want to purchase go on sale, what we refer to in this text as "deal-matching."

CouponMom.com is one of the most useful couponing websites available because it offers a number of different tools that make couponing a whole lot easier. Coupon Mom offers printable coupons directly from their website. The site also offers listings of grocery deals by state, drugstore deals, video tutorials on how to coupon and use the site, restaurant coupons, and other coupon deals available online.

With CouponMom.com, much of the work has already been done for you: site moderators figure out the best deals listed by individual store and state location. If you don't see what you are looking for in the Coupon Mom listings, you can check their publicly available online database of coupon listings using the CouponMom.com system. The system is very simple and starts with the collection of the major coupon circulars in the Sunday paper.

CouponMom.com has databases of all the deals and coupons from the RedPlum (RP), SmartSource (SS), and Procter & Gamble (PG) printed circulars published each week. You can check Coupon Mom's online database for a deal on a specific product and see its corresponding listing in the printed publication. So all you really have to do, instead of perusing all of the individual coupons in the printed circulars, is simply save the circulars every week and use CouponMom.com to zero in on the coupons of interest to you.

CouponMom.com is certainly one of the more robust couponing websites available. However, users should be forewarned that this is a heavily affiliate-based website, meaning that a lot of the site's functionality comes from its partnerships with other sites. CouponMom.com itself is just a heavily search-optimized URL, one that gets good play on Google largely due to the successful publicity efforts of the Coupon Mom herself, Stephanie Nelson.

There's not a whole lot of clear instruction about how to best use the site, and it could be a bit overwhelming for newcomers. There also doesn't appear to be any active community associated with the site. There are no discussion forums to be found, and even the Coupon Mom Facebook page is devoid of much conversation among its nearly half a million subscribers.

Note : Part of the reason for the lack of discussion on the Facebook page is likely Facebook's filtering policy, whereby posts made don't necessarily show up on the news feeds of subscribers.

2. Coupons.com

Featured as a top-three couponing site on Today.com's money section,[18] Coupons.com is one of the most popular coupon websites around. One of the features of Coupons.com is the ability to share coupons with friends via Facebook, Twitter, and email. Also, there are plenty of coupons available directly on the site.

One of the nice things about coupons.com is that you can get a good amount of use out of the site without signing up for a paid membership. A paid membership does, however, grant you access to a separate tier of coupon offers. It's always difficult to determine whether these pay-to-play couponing propositions are worth the expense, since every shopper has different needs and habits. My advice is to start by finding out how far you can get with the freebies before considering any paid membership. Coupons.com and other similar sites are presumably generating promotional revenue from product manufacturers; if they're too intent on collecting direct revenue from the consumer then there is cause to be skeptical about the quality of the service.

---

[18] Louis DeNicola, "Cheapism: Where to find the best coupons online," *Today.com.* (August 2014): Accessed June 1, 2016.

In addition to your traditional grocery coupons, Coupons.com offers coupon codes for online shoppers as well. Many of their deals hinge on your willingness to "like" a particular Facebook page or post in order to qualify for certain coupon offers.

In the often chaotic, distraction-prone world of couponing, Coupons.com, dubbed a "perennial favorite" by the *Today* show, provides a fairly focused experience for the site user and doesn't require a lot of hoop-jumping to print coupons and save money.

3. *GrocerySmarts.com*

GrocerySmarts.com is your one-stop shop for grocery couponing. This site offers printable grocery lists with corresponding coupons for local stores and listings of sale prices. Much like Coupon Mom, Grocery Smarts does much of the couponing work for you so that you don't have to. The downside of Grocery Smarts is that there is a slight learning curve involved in using the site, simply because of the sheer volume of information available. It may take a little time to get used to the site layout and how everything works, but after that, this site will offer significant savings for grocery shopping.

Another thing that we really like about GrocerySmarts.com is its regionalized shopping lists. If you're able to locate one of your favorite local grocery stores, then you'll get access to a full and updated listing of all the sales featured in the current store circular as well as any coupon offers that could provide an even deeper discount. The best part is that Grocery Smarts rates all of the featured sales, so you know which ones are seriously good deals. For the more moderate couponers, using the rating system at Grocery Smarts can be a highly effective starting point for a simplified yet deal-conscious shopping experience.

4. MyCoupons.com

MyCoupons.com offers a search engine that allows you to search for products by product name, store, or keyword. This site also offers printable coupons like several of the others featured in this list, but MyCoupons.com is not as extensive as Coupon Mom or Grocery Smarts. Furthermore, this website doesn't appear to be as frequently updated as some of the others. The second time we dropped in on it, it had virtually no activity on the home page. And the overall selection throughout the site seems dismal compared to that of the more robust sites such as Coupons.com and CouponMom.com. There's certainly no evidence of any community activity (its community link is dead) and there doesn't seem to be any grocery-related content at all.

5. Checkout51.com

Checkout51.com is a well-maintained couponing website that thrives on simplicity. Unlike Coupons.com and similar sites, it doesn't bombard the browser with affiliate content and a multitude of special offers coming from every which way. Instead, Checkout51.com offers a simple yet substantial *grocery list* of items with associated rebates offering anything from fifty cents to three dollars back on your purchases. To redeem with Checkout51.com, you upload your receipt using your camera and wait about an hour for it to be confirmed. Once you've reached twenty dollars' worth of rebates, you can cash out on the website or through the app, and you're sent a check in the mail.

Checkout51.com updates every Thursday with a new list of items that can be rebated. The thing many people prefer about Checkout51.com is that it doesn't expect you to always buy name brands. They have "generic" items such as milk or orange juice or eggs. Any brand you want, just buy milk this week and you get a rebate. This is an especially nice feature. They also reward you with two dollars just for signing up and uploading your first receipt. On top of that, there's a sweepstakes part of the app that gives you a chance to win various gift cards and rewards, just for having a grocery bill over sixty dollars—a good deal considering that, in this day and age, it's nearly impossible not to exceed sixty dollars on one shopping trip.

6. TheKrazyCouponLady.com

This is another site that was recognized by the *Today* show's blog as being one of the most helpful online couponing resources available. After spending some time with the site, we concur. Everything about TheKrazyCouponLady.com is dialed-in, stylish, useful, and exciting. There are nicely made short videos with useful information about couponing and general savings opportunities available at different stores. The site is clean, up to date, and thorough. One thing we really like about this site is how it scours not just coupon clearinghouses (like Valassis and SmartSource) for manufacturer coupons, but also directs site users to coupons published directly on manufacturer websites.

Rather than providing a section for "regional info," TheKrazyCouponLady.com accomplishes the same feat by providing information on a vast assortment of retailers, including grocery companies and a multitude of affiliate brands. You won't have any trouble finding up-to-date information about deals available at your favorite stores.

More Website Evaluation Tips

The aforementioned coupon sites are not the only ones available.

New websites are popping up all the time. Whenever you decide to take advantage of an online resource, there are a few things to keep in mind: coupon variety, feature set, ease of use, and available help and support.

Coupon variety includes both printable coupons and online coupon codes. Sometimes these coupon codes offer great deals on things like free shipping. Next, most coupon sites include similar feature sets; some of these features may include share buttons for social media, advanced search features, online forums, or options for subscribing to newsletters or mailing lists. Ease of use is another important feature to look for; if information on a website is confusing or the site is difficult to navigate, look for deals elsewhere. Finally, available help and support is very important, and it's always a good idea to read a website's FAQ section to aid in taking a proactive approach to using the site.

The Era of Groupon

A write-up on online couponing wouldn't be complete without a mention of Groupon.com. Groupon, which we mentioned in Chapter 1 as an example of "crowd-sourced couponing," has made great strides toward becoming the world's leading coupon source. Groupon.com forwards you weekly updates of deals available in your area. If you're one of the more proactive Groupon users, you can, of course, search for specific Groupon offers that suit your interests. One of the fun and unique features of the Groupon app is a location-based notification function that will alert you when you're in close proximity to a venue or retailer offering a Groupon deal. This alert function is a great choice for couponers who enjoy a dash of spontaneity every now and then.

From concerts to cooking lessons to kids' toys, Groupon offers deep discounts on a variety of goods and services. Customers can get a giant cookie from Great American Cookies for less than half the regular price, or 40 percent off a skydiving lesson. There are also many deals on things that people wouldn't normally think of buying for themselves.

Want to treat a loved one to a full-day spa package? Groupon has local spa deals for up to 60 percent off regular prices.

With Groupon, you select the deal you want and "buy" it on the spot. Once you check out, they send you an email with your e-certificate. Some deals do require 24-hour notice or more, so always be sure to read the fine print. Groupon makes this easy for you by adding a "Fine Print" section in full-sized text for each of their unique offerings.

Groupon and other crowd-sourced coupon offerings may not integrate well into the strategy of couponers motivated by frugality. Not many of the deals offered by Groupon are for practical everyday items like deodorant or breakfast cereal. In fact, it seems the main utility of the Grouponing service is to provide cost-effective ways to get people out of the house. Retailers that use Groupon are often attempting to find a market for an exotic service, such as a themed restaurant, a cryogenic spa, hot yoga, or some other source of fanfare that's off the beaten path. Nevertheless, it's hard to talk about online couponing without mentioning Groupon and the impact it's had on the "deal" economy.

Tip : Set Up a Separate Email Account for Couponing

In the world of online couponing, email addresses are like currency. You can get some amazing offers from clearinghouses, manufacturers, clipping services, bloggers, etc., but many of them are first going to want you to cough up your email address so they can presumably make themselves a permanent fixture in your inbox. You know what? Let them. Go ahead and make like Hillary Clinton and set up a separate email account. Use this email account only for couponing. This will prevent your personal inbox from getting bogged down by the marketers, while giving you access to the deals you're seeking.

To Recap

- The Internet has reshaped the couponing experience by adding more instant access to coupons and information.

- Quick deal-matching, expanded networking, and the rapid proliferation of coupons are the three major advantages that couponers can reap from the Internet.

- The best couponing websites out there may appear complex at first; be patient with yourself as you learn the ropes.

- Groupon has changed the very nature of coupons, but the service may not accommodate couponers principally motivated by frugality.

| 7 |
Couponing Apps & Social Media

In This Chapter
- Ways to strategically employ social media to find great coupons
- The advantages of opening and maintaining separate, dedicated social media accounts purely for couponing purposes
- A review of RetailMeNot and other mobile couponing apps

Social Media Couponing

In recent years, Internet users have taken advantage of popular social media trends in their couponing efforts. Social media platforms like Facebook and Twitter are often tied into product manufacturers' marketing campaigns, and some of the online deals these companies offer are designed to require social media participation. Also, social media may be utilized when trading coupons or coupon codes, or when participating in online discussion forums. Two examples of online couponing websites that are firmly rooted in social media are Groupon (groupon.com), which we've discussed extensively throughout this book, and another crowd-sourced couponing company called Living Social (livingsocial.com). Both sites offer deeply discounted localized deals and encourage their customers to spread the word via social media.

Think of "Likes" & "Follows" as Another Form of Currency

Just as coupons can be treated as a form of currency when used in lieu of actual money, and just as email addresses are often regarded by the marketing world as their own form of currency, it's also helpful to think of Facebook "likes" and "follows" as yet another type of currency that you can proffer up in exchange for great coupons. Many businesses highly value social media visibility and will, on more than a few occasions, offer a substantial incentive for consumers to join their social networks. Every day, promotions are run where a discount, or a free product, or a chance to win a free product are offered in exchange for a Facebook "like."

Success in social media couponing will also require good *monitoring skills*. What good is an amazing offer on that beautiful handbag if you're not scanning your Twitter feed at the right time to catch wind of the promo? For the shopper seeking to maximize social media couponing opportunities, monitoring is key. You can start by setting up a new folder on the bookmarks bar of your browser and loading it up with your targeted company's social media pages. For example, if you're a big fan of Louis Vuitton and never want to miss a promotion, then you'd create a new bookmark folder and fill it with the following URLs:

- https://twitter.com/louisvuitton
- https://www.instagram.com/louisvuitton/
- https://www.facebook.com/LouisVuitton/
- https://www.linkedin.com/company/louis-vuitton

Note : Not to say that Louis Vuitton is particularly prone to issuing great coupons (thriftiness isn't generally considered a part of their appeal) but there are hundreds of thousands of companies out there that on any given day would gladly trade an amazing deal for a "like" or a "follow."

Most browsers allow you to right-click on a folder full of bookmarks and select "open all bookmarks." In this way you can efficiently keep tabs (no pun intended) on possible offers and coupons issued or promoted through social media.

In addition to checking in regularly with your favorite retailers, you can also monitor the interwebs for coupon offers by searching through hashtags. Typing in "#coupons" in the Twitter search bar will pull up a whole slew of up-to-the-minute offers from all over the Internet. You can do the same with Instagram. In fact, at the time of this writing, if you do a search for "#coupons" in Instagram you'll immediately get an offer from Lyft (a competitor of the chauffeuring service Uber) for a $50 ride credit.

As you transition from website-based utilities, such as those discussed in Chapter 6, to social utilities, you will notice that the types of offers you come across may be well off the beaten path in promoting interesting goods and services that you won't find in the Sunday newspaper insert.

If you're not concerned much about brands (like Louis Vuitton) but are instead looking for a coupon on a particular product or service, then simply tailor your bookmarking or hashtags to target social media pages and accounts likely to offer coupons for your sought-after amenity.

Note : Pinterest and Instagram have recently become more popular with coupon users and coupon manufacturers.

Open New Social Media Accounts for Couponing

Here's your chance to put that nickname from high school to good use. A lot of people are reluctant to use their primary social media account to like, follow, and post a bunch of marketing content, even if it means capitalizing on great deals. Remember how we set up a dedicated couponing email account in the previous chapter? Let's do the same thing here.

In order to get maximum value out of social media couponing, you don't want to have to worry about annoying your friends with marketing retweets and timeline posts. With your new account you'll be able to post, share, and participate at-will without annoying anyone, except the other couponers you'll follow and friend with your new online identity. That's right, we wouldn't want you to start your journey as a social couponer without any friends. Use the search bars built into the social media platforms to find people and companies that share your newfound passion for coupon-scouring the interwebs. Find other people who list couponing and shopping as their hobbies. There are others out there like you. They're just waiting for you to reach out and make first contact.

Social Media Coupon Networking

Once you have your dedicated social couponing accounts set up, you'll be in the perfect position to start building a serious online network to assist in your endeavors. "Friend" or "follow" anyone seriously involved in couponing. Often these individuals will openly share links to deals and coupons on their Twitter or Facebook pages, providing you with links to deals that you may be interested in (it may be worth adding their social media URLs to your bookmarks).

If you're a frequent customer at a particular restaurant or bar, then be sure to also frequent their Facebook and Twitter pages, especially before you head out for a visit. They may have just posted an awesome deal that you'd never have known about otherwise. Businesses will often offer these same-day deals exclusively on their social media sites. They are also inclined to offer coupons and rewards for "likes" or "shares." Show your support on social media and they'll respond in kind. I've seen many major marketing campaigns, offered by restaurants, small businesses, and even major corporations, specifically aimed at rewarding their followers with giveaways. If you're in the market for a certain product, take some time to scout relevant social media forums. You'll be surprised by how much you can save in "real time" just by staying vigilant.

If you're the type, like me, who usually tries to avoid incorporating social media into any activity that demands focus, then take comfort in the fact that you'll be using your dedicated couponing accounts, not your personal accounts. That means that you're not going to be interrupted by a funny video from your best friend while you're trying to plan your shopping trip. You can watch the video when you get back.

More on Networking

Throughout this book, we've continuously pointed out the value of maintaining a healthy couponing network. You don't have to coupon all alone, nor should you. Networking with other couponers, whether through social media or face-to-face, is often the best way to find the really good deals. Much in the way that consignment or book loaning clubs evolve, couponing groups can have the same benefit. Making friends with other couponers can be mutually beneficial and a great time-saver. There's nothing like putting a call out to all your coupon friends when you need to save on diapers or your third gallon of milk that week.

One great way to network is by searching for "coupon databases" online. There are many different niches and no site specifically titled "Coupon Database." It's generally a page on other blogs or sites. These are pages where all coupon-savvy participants upload coupons and tips they've found. Many are printable and some are downloadable. They're also rated in many cases, for how easy they are to use and whether all stores in that chain will take them. Some of the sites you find will even have an app.

You do have to be careful because, since some of the sites are specialized, often by geography, not all stores have to participate. You must always read the fine print.

Online Message Boards

Speaking of networking, message boards and online forums are a great place to exchange information regarding coupons and deals for specific stores or products. Before participating in online forums, make sure to read any applicable FAQs regarding rules or prohibited posting material.

The following common abbreviations are used frequently in coupon message boards:

- **CC** : Concealed Cash – (cash in an envelope)
- **Envie** : Envelope
- **FSOT** : For Sale or Trade – (a deal that someone is willing to sell or trade)
- **GC** : Gift Card – (people often trade gift cards for cash value, coupons, and other deals)
- **H** : Have
- **ISO** : In Search Of
- **Potluck** : An envelope with a mixture of coupons someone is willing to sell or trade
- **PP** : PayPal
- **RAOK** : Random Acts of Kindness
- **W** : Want

Mobile App-Based Couponing

Mobile couponing tools are some of the most useful tools you can use during your couponing efforts. Since these tools run on your mobile phone or tablet, you can use them while at the store as well. When looking for mobile couponing apps, the first thing to do is make a list of all the stores you usually frequent. Then, check and see if these stores offer a mobile application at your device's app store. For example, some stores that offer mobile apps include Target, Walgreens, and CVS.

Other popular mobile apps for couponing include the following:

1. RetailMeNot

This Austin-based company (RetailMeNot Inc.) is the undisputed heavyweight champion of couponing apps. The site was responsible for some \$4.8 billion worth of discounted transactions in 2015.[19] The app's functionality is very simple. Its extensive partnership with thousands of retailers allows users to conduct coupon searches through the app on-site. The value of the app is that it can be summoned during virtually any shopping trip, and odds are you will discover that the retailer you're visiting has a coupon featured in the app. It's this unique level of on-site responsiveness, coupled with a smooth user interface and a stunningly broad retail partnership base, that makes RetailMeNot a huge winner in the field of couponing apps.

2. Cellfire

Cellfire is a mobile app that was brought to market by Catalina, the now-famous couponing company that's behind the systems that create instant coupons for customers at checkout. Cellfire is perhaps the best in its space for grocery coupons. You use the app by connecting it to your grocery store's rewards card (you can connect multiple rewards cards from various stores) and the app will automatically direct you to coupons that complement the grocery store's current offerings. You select the coupons that you want to use, and when you're at the grocery store, simply tap on "saved coupons" to ensure you're getting the right products.

3. SnipSnap

This app allows you to take a picture of a printed coupon and uses character recognition to store the name and expiration date of the coupon within the app. Once the coupon is stored, you can use it at checkout just as you'd use a mobile coupon. It also has an option for sharing coupons through social media. Unfortunately, as of this writing, SnipSnap does not work with manufacturer coupons.

---

[19] "investor.retailmenot.com," *RetailMeNot.com*, Accessed June 1, 2016.

4. Shopkick

Use this app to browse specific store deals and rewards.

5. Yowza

This app automatically informs you of deals at stores in your local geographical area. When you are ready to check out at a store, simply have the cashier scan the coupon barcode on your smartphone screen using this app.

6. Grocery Smarts

Grocery Smarts is good for helping you organize your coupons within a single app. Much of the difficult cross-reference couponing work is automatically done for you with this app. In combination with its website (discussed in Chapter 6) the Grocery Smarts app can hugely accelerate your path to becoming an excellent couponer.

7. CardStar

From the makers of the email marketing platform Constant Contact, this app takes on the crises of keychains and wallets overloaded with rewards cards from every shop in town. CardStar allows you to move all of your store rewards cards to a single application. Not only will you lighten your wallet, but you'll also be able to use the app to keep track of your rewards points and the other various perks you earn from each retailer you frequent.

8. Ibotta.com

Ibotta is a couponing app available on iPhone and Android systems. You download the app to your phone and click the registration link that it sends to your email. Once registered, you receive weekly updates that tell you which products are available at a discount. You purchase the items you need and scan the receipt with your phone's camera. Once uploaded, the receipt is verified and your rebates are applied to your account. You can redeem your earnings in the form of cash sent directly to your PayPal account, or you can choose from a selection of gift cards from retailers such as Starbucks, Redbox, and iTunes.

Ibotta also has many ways of earning more discounts through the app usage itself. There are surveys to take and videos to watch. Also, you get points every time you link your app to your social media account. Just bought a carton of ice cream that will earn you seventy-five cents back? Tweet it and earn another fifty cents!

To Recap

- Think of "likes" and "follows" as a type of free currency that you can spend in return for great offers from your favorite retailers.

- Use searchable hashtags, such as #coupons, to find deals on social media.

- Don't be shy; connect with other couponers via social media to share coupons and tips.

- People have more success with new pursuits when they use the buddy system; build your network, lean on it, contribute to it, love it!

- RetailMeNot is currently the best general couponing app available; Cellfire is probably the most simplified utility for grocery shopping.

| 8 |

Nonconventional Couponing

In This Chapter

- Innovative money-saving consumer apps and other utilities that don't use coupons (per se)

We added this chapter for couponers who are interested in exploring ways of saving money by using methods and tools that extend beyond conventional couponing. We figure that if you're already going to learn how to use couponing apps and websites, then you'll be ideally suited to leverage some of these nonconventional money-saving utilities.

1. Lucktastic

Lucktastic is one of those apps that lets you cure two obsessions at once. If you love lottery scratch-off tickets, then you've found your app! There are a few different ways to win with this unconventional app. First, you scratch different "cards" for chances to win points and even cash. Each card has a bonus square that gives you points, even if you didn't win in the traditional sense.

You can do other small things for points, like with most apps. If you share your love for Lucktastic with Facebook or Twitter, you get points. If you refer a friend, you get points. If you watch advertiser videos (commercials) between cards, you get points.

These points all add up to some incredible rewards. You can choose to redeem any cash prizes through Dwolla.com, a partner company.

The points can be redeemed through gift cards to retail chains like Target or Amazon. You can even earn movie tickets for your points. Additionally, if you choose to push your luck, the app has three bonus scratch-off cards that you can purchase with points. The bonus cards give higher payouts than regular cards. Your points can also be used to enter into raffle drawings for things like television sets and even vehicles!

2. Mobile Performance Meter

The Mobile Performance Meter is not your standard run-of-the-mill mobile app, but it can be a great way to earn easy rewards. The app is downloaded and acts as a widget, running in the background. You begin with 100 points and earn 20 points per day, just for letting the app run on your phone. Then, at various times, surveys will pop up. If you complete the surveys you earn points. Once you've earned at least 500 points you can redeem them for gift cards.

Participating retailers include Barnes & Noble, Amazon, Target, and many others. At last count, fifty different retailers had partnered with the app. You receive your gift card in the form of an e-certificate that's emailed to you. Simple as that.

For those with reservations about any type of "tracking" app, do download at your own risk. This app is described as a Nielsen-box-style tracker (the boxes used to assign ratings to television programs) except it tracks data usage instead of television interests. The first survey you take after downloading the app relates to your opinions about your current mobile provider. All of your feedback is anonymous, and your personal information is never requested.

3. *Debit & Credit Cards*

One of the ways in which banks throw their weight around is by providing gifts to their customers to reward specific behaviors. These rewards are often based on the purchase of certain types of goods, such as groceries or gasoline. Consumers who prefer not to dramatically alter their spending habits in response to incentives can still easily profit in certain situations. For instance, Bank of America offers its customers cash-back deals that are specifically informed by purchases that the customer has already made. While reviewing their online statements, customers will be able to explore these special cash-back offers that have been tailored to complement their existing spending habits. For instance, if you use your card a lot at Starbucks, you may find a cashback offer promoting the purchase of Starbucks coffee from Target.

Other credit cards offer similar savings opportunities, like cash back on gas or groceries, with no other strings attached. Those one to five percent returns can add up fast, and you really don't consciously have to do anything different.

For those willing to alter their routines for the sake of a bargain, rewards-based bank cards can be a great way to find new restaurants and stores you wouldn't have otherwise discovered or tried out. My father, who's now been mentioned multiple times in this book, strives to use his credit cards as much as possible for purchases, reaping the rewards while religiously paying off the entirety of his statement balances each month (not just the minimum payment). This strategy is a sound one financially, as long as you can safely count yourself among the approximately 30 percent of credit card users who clear their balances in full each month, so as to avoid any interest payments. Paying interest to your credit card company will, of course, quickly cancel out any rewards earnings.

4. *Surveys & Deal Pitches*

Disney, for one, has this great sales pitch that really works. If you call their toll-free number and listen to them describe the Disney Princess Cruise, or whatever they're promoting, you can get deeply discounted admission tickets. They surely can't be the only ones doing this, and it's a perfect win–win situation. You're in the market for whatever product or service these companies are selling, plus you get a much better discount than you would in a traditional manner. It works much like the "time-share" package pitches worked in the '80s. But at least this way you're picking something you already wanted to buy.

Even if you're not afraid of saying, "No thank you on the time share, but I'll keep the free gifts," and even if you're handy with your Outlook or iCalendar and surely won't forget to call in and cancel your "promotional" service after thirty days, it may *still* prove useful to do some front-end research before you attempt to scam the scammers. I recently thought I had a clear-cut path to sixty dollars in rebates from a company called Great Fun, which offers the rebates in exchange for trying their "service" for thirty days. I made a note on my calendar to call in and cancel twenty-eight days after signing up. I did so. And I waited. Eventually I got a note in the mail that said my rebates were denied because I'd failed to send in an accompanying receipt for my purchase. Funny thing is, I'm a fairly detail-oriented person, and I'd happily bet away all my buffalo pennies that the instructions I received didn't mention anything about printing out a receipt (Great Fun is an online company, so there was never any paper receipt issued after I signed up). Between going through the initial pitch and then the cancellation (where they offered me a special low subscription rate at only a fraction of the cost), and now having to dig into my email to try to find this mysterious "receipt," I feel I've earned that sixty dollars and then some. Had I taken more time to read over the reviews of Great Fun, I may have been aware that I was soon to play the cat to Great Fun's mouse.

5. No More Rack/Overstock

These companies have apps and Facebook pages dedicated to deeply discounted goods. You don't need a paper or mobile coupon to buy these items. Check periodically with the wholesalers for their deal updates and save tremendously on items you were going to purchase anyway. Usually larger chains will oversupply certain items, and then send them to these stores when sales wane. Think of it as the next step beyond outlet stores.

6. Ebates

Ebates, and other companies like it, are picking off the rest of the wholesale materials and letting you bid on items with a chance of getting huge discounts. Since Amazon and Ebay have become so popular, many sites like Ebates have popped up. If yours is the winning bid, then you really can buy electronics and big-ticket items at 90 percent discounts. The trick is to watch for predatory sites that request more personal information than they should. Ebates, and other reputable sites, use PayPal and other off-site money transaction companies to ensure a triple-blind purchase process. Be sure your wholesaler or auction site is legitimate before being distracted by shiny objects on their pages.

To Recap

- In the era of the "app" and with such a high premium on marketing data, there are countless money-saving opportunities available to consumers.

conclusion

As with anything, people can get a bit out of hand with couponing. The *Extreme Couponing* television show feeds into that hysteria, but it can still provide helpful tips, even for the more moderate couponer.

Not everyone has time to scour seven newspapers and the entire Internet for coupons and deals. So here are a few tips that will help you save, without costing more of your sanity.

- **DON'T BUY A PRODUCT JUST BECAUSE YOU HAVE A COUPON!** This is a huge mistake that many people make. If you don't need it, don't buy it. You won't save money that way. And you'll end up with a garage full of things you "might" need one day. Hoard much?

- Don't drive across town to save twenty cents on one item. Really. How is that productive?

- Pre-shop your favorite stores to check who has the lowest prices on your couponed items. Many local stores will have the same things on sale as their competition, but often someone's got the edge over their neighbor.

- Check in-store flyers. There are often "meal deals" where you buy a large lasagna and get a soda, bread, and ice cream for free. Dinner, anyone?

- Membership discount stores like Sam's Club and Costco have bonus perks once a month. If you're a member, time your shopping trip accordingly.

- Know your store's routine. After tracking who has what on sale when, you can time your trips to coincide with the big sales.

- Know the regular prices for things in your area. Just because something says BOGO (buy one get one) are you really getting the second for free? Or is the first one priced higher than normal? Beware of these tactics.

- Box stores like Save-A-Lot and Aldi are popping up everywhere and giving Sam's Club and Costco a run for their money. These places make you bag your own groceries, but the savings are incredible. Many people prefer these stores because not only are you saving, but you aren't forced to buy only name-brand items. Imagine how much you can save by buying a giant box of store-brand chocolate cereal versus using a coupon for twenty-five cents off a name brand.

- Meat markets can save you a lot of money if you find the right store. Stocking up on the large meat packs and then using the BOGO deals at your local grocer could have your family eating like kings for the entire month. Just beware of cleanliness. It's not such a great deal on hamburger meat if your family can't keep said meat down!

- Also with meat markets, watch the family package deals. Don't buy something with turkey necks and gizzards if you don't know how to cook them, or don't want to. Find a store, and a meat pack, that fits your family's tastes. They are out there!

- If you get meat packs or "frozen" packs at other wholesalers, do the math. Figure what you're paying per pound or per meal for these deals before deciding to buy. Sometimes the coupon or BOGO at your local store will come out cheaper this week.

- Rate apps! Read the ratings of others. Be honest. Don't waste your time on apps or coupon banks that don't deliver, and help your fellow couponer avoid the same mistake. It will help thin the herd and keep reputable apps in business.

- Don't drive yourself crazy trying to save that extra penny. Of course, it can be tempting and, at times, necessary, but not at the expense of your friends and family. Don't end up on a new reality show called *Extreme Coupon Hoarders!*

Couponing takes work and organization, but the rewards are huge! I am confident that the knowledge and strategies presented in this book, coupled with a personal determination to succeed, will save you thousands of dollars, even in your first year of couponing.

glossary

BOGO
Buy one, get one free

Catalina
Named after the Catalina Company, referring to coupons that are automatically printed at checkout following a purchase

Circulars
Small magazine-sized publications issued by grocers (featuring sales, "grocery circulars") and by coupon clearinghouses (featuring coupons, "coupon circulars")

Coupon Clearinghouse
An intermediary company that issues coupons on behalf of manufacturers and guarantees retailers payment for coupons collected

Coupon Information Corporation
A private interest group that maintains a database of known fraudulent coupons

Direct Marketing Association
A trade organization that oversees the chains of communication between marketers and consumers

Double Couponing
Promotions run by grocery stores where they agree to match the value of manufacturer coupons, yielding double the discount for the customer

IP
Shorthand for Internet printable coupons

Item Recording
A self-assessment process whereby a customer records (writes down) the mix of his typical grocery purchase

Manufacturer Coupons
Coupons issued by a manufacturer of a product, theoretically redeemable wherever said product is sold

OYNO
On your next order

PG
Shorthand for Procter & Gamble

Printed Coupons
Coupons available in print

Stacking
The simultaneous use of a manufacturer coupon and a store-issued coupon

Stockpiling
Using duplicate coupons to purchase multiple units of a specific product at a favorable price

Store Coupons
Coupons issued by a retailer and only redeemable at said retailer's store location

RP
Shorthand for RedPlum, a coupon clearinghouse and an issuer of circulars

SS
Shorthand for SmartSource, a coupon clearinghouse and an issuer of circulars

about clydebank

We are a multi-media publishing company that provides reliable, high-quality, and easily accessible information to a global customer base. Developed out of the need for beginner-friendly content that can be accessed across multiple platforms, we deliver unbiased, up-to-date, information through our multiple product offerings.

Through our strategic partnerships with some of the world's largest retailers, we are able to simplify the learning process for customers around the world, providing our readers with an authoritative source of information for the subjects that matter to them. Our end-user focused philosophy puts the satisfaction of our customers at the forefront of our mission. We are committed to creating multi-media products that allow our customers to learn what they want, when they want, and how they want.

ClydeBank Finance is a division of the multimedia-publishing firm ClydeBank Media. ClydeBank Media's goal is to provide affordable, accessible information to a global market through different forms of media such as eBooks, paperback books and audio books. Company divisions are based on subject matter, each consisting of a dedicated team of researchers, writers, editors and designers.

For more information, please visit us at :
www.clydebankmedia.com
or contact info@clydebankmedia.com

Your world, simplified.

notes

WANT FREE AUDIOBOOKS?

connecting authors & readers

HOW DOES IT WORK?

sign up　　　　**select book**

get email　　　　**read & review**

1. Sign-up by visiting www.revizea.com/signup and select what types of books you are interested in receiving.

2. You'll receive weekly e-mails from Revizea listing the latest titles available to you for free.

3. Select a title and format (print, ebook, or audiobook) by completing the corresponding online form.

4. Await confirmation that your request has been approved (approximately 24 hours.)

5. Receive your title, read (or listen), and leave a review.

IMPORTANT:

Your review must include a disclaimer stating that you received the product for free in exchange for a honest and unbiased review.

Get a *FREE* ClydeBank Media Audiobook + 30 Day Free Trial to Audible.com

Get titles like this absolutely free :

- *Business Plan Quickstart Guide*
- *Options Trading Quickstart Guide*
- *ITIL For Beginners*
- *Scrum Quickstart Guide*
- *JavaScript Quickstart Guide*
- *3D Printing Quickstart Guide*

- *LLC Quickstart Guide*
- *Lean Six Sigma Quickstart Guide*
- *Project Management QuickStart Guide*
- *Social Security Simplified*
- *Medicare Simplified*
- *and more!*

To Sign Up & Get your Free Audiobook, visit :
www.clydebankmedia.com/audible-trial

3/17

UNION COUNTY PUBLIC LIBRARY
316 E. Windsor St., Monroe, NC 28112

CPSIA information can be obtained
at www.ICGtesting.com
Printed in the USA
LVOW13s1951220217
525093LV00010B/1017/P